Books are to be returned on or before
the last date below.

RIGHTS
AND WRONGS

RIGHTS AND WRONGS

Coercion, Punishment and the State

DAVID A. HOEKEMA

Selinsgrove: Susquehanna University Press
London and Toronto: Associated University Presses

Associated University Presses
440 Forsgate Drive
Cranbury, NJ 08512

Associated University Presses
25 Sicilian Avenue
London WC1A 2QH, England

Associated University Presses
2133 Royal Windsor Drive
Unit 1
Mississauga, Ontario
Canada L5J 1K5

The paper used in this publication meets the requirements
of the American National Standard for Permanence of Paper
for Printed Library Materials Z39.48-1984.

Library of Congress Cataloging-in-Publication Data

Hoekema, David A.
  Rights and wrongs.

  Bibliography: p.
  Includes index.
  1. Legitimacy of governments.   2. Authority.
3. Punishment.   4. State, The.   I. Title.
JC328.2.H63   1986   320'.01'1   84-40809
ISBN 0-941664-07-4 (alk. paper)

Printed in the United States of America

To Susan Bosma Hoekema,
my interlocutor,
severest critic, and closest friend

CONTENTS

ACKNOWLEDGMENTS

It is my duty and a pleasure to acknowledge the generous assistance of friends and colleagues who have read portions of this work at various stages and who have suggested ways in which it could be improved. It was in the course of conversations with Charles R. Beitz that the plan of the work first took shape in my mind, and he has been a careful and helpful reader of substantial portions of the text. Time constraints prevented me, however, from acting on his suggestion that the entire study should be rewritten in blank verse.

My former colleagues in the Philosophy Department at St. Olaf College have discussed the ideas contained here on many occasions, and I am particularly grateful for the specific suggestions given me by Frederick Stoutland and Edward Langerak. I am deeply indebted, personally as well as philosophically, to my mentors, sometime colleagues, and friends in the Philosophy Department at Calvin College, including Nicholas Wolterstorff, Alvin Plantinga, Peter DeVos, Richard Mouw, Clifton Orlebeke, and Kenneth Konyndyk, for showing me what it means to be dedicated to one's calling as a philosopher and as a Christian. I hope that I am beginning to live up to the ideal which they planted in my mind.

My understanding of the calling of the philosopher was also enriched by my teachers at Princeton University. Gregory Vlastos, Margaret Wilson, Arthur Szathmary, and others with whom I worked in areas outside political philosophy will find few specific ideas in the present work which arose from the seminars they taught, but I hope they will perceive the ways in which their example as philosophers and teachers has deepened my own understanding and commitment. T. M. Scanlon, Jr., who guided my study of political philosophy at Princeton University, deserves my deepest thanks: he has read the manuscript of the present work, which was submitted in a different form as a doctoral dissertation under his supervision, with greater care and patience than could reasonably have been expected of anyone. His suggestions at each stage have been of considerable help in clarifying the development of the argument.

Portions of the present work have been presented at conferences and colloquia in recent years, and the criticisms of commentators and audiences have frequently helped me reformulate my ideas more clearly. Insightful comments on some portions of the work were given to me by Jan Narveson and James P. Sterba.

Susan Bosma Hoekema has been patient past human telling in enduring the demands made upon our relationship and upon my family during the writing of the present study. Her companionship has contributed immeasurably to my own intellectual growth, and her trenchant criticisms of early drafts were all too often well founded.

I am grateful also to my children, Janna and Nicolas, both of them younger than this project, for having helped to remind me daily that life is more than writing philosophy.

David A. Hoekema

RIGHTS
AND WRONGS

1
INTRODUCTION

The task of the political philosopher is to philosophize about politics: to apply the tools of philosophical inquiry and analysis to questions concerning the legitimacy of political institutions and the laws and policies which they make.

The modern state, however, presents a bewildering variety of faces to any inquirer. Among the telephone listings in the Minneapolis telephone book for the federal government alone are the Department of Agriculture (with four columns of subheadings, from "Poultry and Dairy Quality Division" to "St. Anthony Falls Hydraulic Laboratory"), the Central Intelligence Agency, the Coast Guard Mobile Boating Safety Detachment, the Commodity Futures Trading Commission, the Comptroller of the Currency, the Consumer Products Safety Commission, the Department of Defense (three columns of subheadings), the Farm Credit Administration, the Federal Mediation and Reconciliation Service, the Internal Revenue Service, the Occupational Safety and Health Administration, the Bureau of Sport Fisheries and Wildlife, the Upper Mississippi River Basin Commission, and the Veterans Administration.

Faced with such a bewildering diversity of roles and functions, the political philosopher must of necessity begin by a process of abstraction and simplification. In order to assess the moral justification of the activity of the state it is necessary first to identify the essential and characteristic features of political institutions. Many political philosophers have chosen to focus on questions of *distribution* of goods and services in society. Nearly every facet of governmental activity involves in one way or another an alteration in patterns of property holdings. A theory of justice in distribution thus can provide a broadly applicable standard by which the justice of practices and institutions can be judged.

To focus on justice in distribution is to take as central to political philosophy the question, "Who should have what?" Such an approach responds to a challenge to the justice of an existing order which arises from allegations of unfairness in the distribution of property and wealth. The importance of this question for a theory of political justice cannot be denied, and the challenge based on claims of unfairness demands a careful and clearly supported answer. Yet there is another challenge to the justice of governmental practices and institutions, one which strikes more deeply into the very nature of government and which is in a sense conceptually prior to any question of distribution. That challenge has to do with the very concept of political power, including the power to coerce. It is a challenge not only to the justice of governmental institutions and practices but to the legitimacy of government itself.

This more fundamental challenge arises from the recognition that the use of coercion is essential to the nature of the state and that the power of government is intrinsically and inescapably a coercive power. Other institutions may also wield coercive power, to be sure. But the state holds a unique and exclusive authority to coerce. Characteristic of government is the authority to compel compliance with laws and regulations. Rules and laws carry penalties for their violation, and government implicitly or explicitly threatens those who fail to comply with the imposition of these penalties. This is an important respect in which the Veterans Administration and the Bureau of Sport Fisheries and Wildlife differ from voluntary organizations such as the Veterans of Foreign Wars and the Lions Club.

Government has the authority as well as the power to coerce. Interactions between government and individuals, even when they involve no overt force or coercive threats, take place against the background of coercive threats to those who do not comply. According to Max Weber's account, a monopoly on the legitimate use of force within a certain territory is a defining condition of the state.[1] Use of actual force, however, is inessential: a state may govern effectively without resorting to physical force if it is able to bring about order through the threat of its use. Coercion is essential to a political order, even if it does not lead to use of force.

Many of the influences of government on the lives of individuals are exercised not through overt coercion but through more complex and indirect channels. Nevertheless, the government would not be a government if it did not hold the authority to compel compliance. The legitimacy of government depends crucially on the moral justifiability of its use of coercive means.

The challenge to the state's authority which is our concern in this study, therefore, is a challenge to the very existence of the state: it is, in other words, the challenge of anarchism. In the anarchist's judgment, the power of the state is so liable to abuse, so likely to undermine the freedom and welfare of individuals, that such power should not be granted to any social institution. In a just society, the anarchist argues, there would be no government. Instead, the purposes which government now serves would be achieved—more effectively and more justly—by voluntary institutions and associations.[2]

The use of coercion is, on the anarchist view, the essential element of governmental power which makes it illegitimate. Governmental coercion, it is held, leads inevitably to oppression and denial of individual rights. The central thesis of the present study might be summed up as an answer to the anarchist's objection: I will argue that coercion is not intrinsically immoral but, on the contrary, is a necessary part of a just social order. There is a moral presumption against coercion, I will argue, which must be overridden by more urgent moral reasons if coercion is to be morally defended in particular circumstances. But the moral theory that grounds the presumption against coercion—a theory of the nature and structure of individual rights—can also provide the basis for an account of the circumstances under which coercion is justified.

Because coercion is essential to the power of government, in this study we will use the concept of coercion as a lens through which to examine the proper activities of government. Whatever else governments do, they employ coercion; so an account of coercion is a necessary element in a complete theory of the state. Furthermore, the ethical problems raised by coercion are uniquely interesting and challenging problems because of the place which coercion occupies in relation to other modes of interpersonal influence. Governments may influence individuals through many noncoercive means such as persuasion, admonition, and suggestion, but the use of such means is not of such urgent moral concern as is the use of coercion. For an attempt to persuade someone is not a prima facie moral wrong, as is an attempt to coerce her. On the other hand, to coerce someone does not typically involve the actual use of violence against her, and it is a less drastic interference with a person to influence her behavior by coercion than by physically attacking her. There are circumstances in which the use of coercion appears defensible even though actual use of force would not be justified. The moral grounds for coercion therefore appear to be broader than those for the use of force.

The account of the justification of coercion that will be offered here is not intended to provide a moral assessment of noncoercive activities of governments as well. To what extent governments are justified in influencing individuals through persuasion, suggestion, selective disclosure of information, and a host of other means is a question which lies beyond the boundaries of the present study. Nevertheless I believe the account that will be offered of the justification of coercion will be helpful in answering that subsequent question. Indeed, it may be an overstatement to call these two different questions: because of the wide-reaching and highly effective means of communication available to modern governments, and because of their pervasive effect on all aspects of life, it may be impossible to identify instances of governmental influence on individuals which are not, if not in obvious then in more subtle ways, at bottom coercive.

Before we can discuss the morality of coercion, we need to have an account of what coercion is. The next two chapters are therefore devoted to the definitional and analytic question of when it is correct to say that one person has coerced another. In the two chapters following I explore the consequences of coercion for moral and legal responsibility and for freedom of action. I then undertake to account for the moral status of coercion—why coercion is presumptively wrong and what circumstances can justify its use. The concept of *rights* is crucial in the assessment of coercion, and the observations that will be offered concerning the grounding and the structure of rights will illuminate the reasons why coercion is presumptively wrong as well as the reasons which sometimes override this presumption. The theory of coercion and rights is applied in the last two chapters of the present study to a specific area of application: the justification of societal institutions of punishment.

Some limits on the scope of this study will already have become evident. As I have mentioned, I shall concentrate on the use of coercion by the state rather than on other means of influencing behavior. Furthermore, although I shall make reference at times, especially in exploring the concept of coercion, to coercion of one individual by another, my primary interest is in the use of coercion in the state, as exercised by office-holders in government on individual citizens.

Before proceeding with our exploration of the concept of coercion, it may be helpful to say a word about terminology. A *society*, as I shall use the term, is a body of persons residing in a certain area, united by a complex web of relationships. Predominant among these relationships is usually a single structure of political authority and subordination. In most societies there is one political system according to which some persons have the power to give orders, to enact or enforce laws, to collect taxes, to issue licenses, and the like; and some or all persons are required to obey commands made by those who hold authority. When a society has such a unifying political structure, we may call it a *state*.

Government is the political structure of a society, the system whereby some hold political authority. A government is a particular body of persons who at a given time hold and exercise political power. Those subject to political authority are the *members* of the society. They may be called the *citizens* of the state, in recognition of their place in the structure of political power, but this is imprecise: "citizens" is commonly applied only to those who have certain rights and privileges which not all residents may have. Further, it is inappropriate to speak of "citizens" of an absolutist monarchy in which neither the derivation of political authority nor the establishment of law is held to have anything to do with the will of individuals not in power. The members of a society are also referred to as *subjects* of the government, but this seems inappropriate in a society that conceives of itself as a democracy.

Although precision in terms is desirable, I do not believe that very much importance should be attached to the use of these terms. A dispute over their meaning is likely to be grounded in substantive disagreement and is not likely to be resolved by clarification of terms, much less by stipulative definition.[3]

Notes

1. Max Weber, *The Theory of Social and Economic Organization*, trans. A. M. Henderson and Talcott Parsons (New York: The Free Press, 1974), 154.

2. This account of anarchism is no more than an oversimplified sketch, and I have not attempted to take note of the sharp differences among defenders of anarchism concerning the immorality of government. Michail Bakunin, at one extreme, champions revolution as the only remedy for the intolerable oppression of government; William Godwin, whose Enlightenment faith in human reason places him at the other extreme on many issues, condemns revolution under any circumstances but calls for the gradual displacement of government, valuable as it is in some respects, by the unimpeded exercise of private judgment. Both of these writers share with other anarchists, nevertheless, a fundamental moral disapproval of the coercive power of government. See G. P. Maximoff, ed., *The Political Philosophy of Bakunin* (Glencoe, Ill.: Free Press, 1953); William Godwin, *Enquiry Concerning Political Justice* (Toronto: University of Toronto Press, 1946).

3. My account of the meaning of "state" and "society" is similar to that of Ernest Barker, in *Principles of Political and Social Theory* (Oxford: Clarendon Press, 1951), Bk. II. Barker uses "society" and "state" as extensionally equivalent terms, the former referring to the numerous nonobligatory social organizations of a nation, the latter to its political structure. Although this comes close to the difference between state and society, to use the two terms coextensively seems to me rather confusing. More important, I find some of Barker's claims about the distinction— e.g., that membership in the groups that constitute society is always voluntary, and that the state has a single purpose—to be oversimplifications.

2
COERCION AND RELATED CONCEPTS

The general topic of the present study, it has been suggested above, is the relationship between the individual and the state. That relationship is characteristically one in which the great preponderance of force and control lies in the hands of the state, for the state wields extensive powers of coercion over the individuals subject to its authority. In order to undertake an ethical study of the relationship between individual and state, therefore, we must begin by giving an account of the nature and the justifiability of coercion. The present chapter will prepare the way for a definition of coercion by exploring the relation between coercion and several related means of influencing behavior. In the chapter following I will set coercion apart from these other means of influence, and lay the groundwork for further discussion of the moral status of coercion, by suggesting a definition of coercion which differs from the accounts that others have offered.

What, then, is coercion? We may begin to take aim at the target of our inquiry by observing that there are some contexts in which coercion cannot occur. An inanimate object, for example, cannot be coerced. We cannot speak—except metaphorically—of coercing a stone or an automobile. The computer on which I have prepared this manuscript cannot be deterred from following out the inexorable logic that governs its internal processes by threats or maledictions, however severe, as I have too often had occasion to observe.

If I threaten a dog with a stick, on the other hand, I may well succeed in keeping the animal out of my yard. It seems appropriate to call this an example of coercion, and it seems therefore that animals can sometimes be coerced. Yet to speak of coercion in this context is to attribute to the dog a decision to stay away rather than risk a beating. To speak of coercing animals, then, requires us to interpret their behavior as voluntary.

Coercion is exercised above all over persons. In the case of persons as of animals, to speak of the application of coercion presupposes that the coerced agent has willful control over her behavior. A person cannot be coerced to have a fever, though she can be coerced to act as if she had one. I can be forced to stop breathing but not to stop my pulse. But coerced acts are unlike other voluntary acts in that they are responses to others' threats.

Let us begin to draw the lines around the category of coercion more precisely: To coerce someone is to force him to perform an act or to restrain him from an act. Coerced acts are acts that a person is induced to perform by threats. Although they are acts over which the person has voluntary control, they are performed under compulsion. Coerced acts are not unintentional: a person who hands over his money to a stranger rather than submit to a beating does so intentionally. He knows what he is doing and prefers to give up his money rather than undergo a beating. But although his act results from his choice, he can choose only among a restricted set of available alternatives that has been imposed on him by another person.

The foregoing is a rough and approximate account of coercion, and each of the features mentioned—compulsion, intentionality, the restriction of available alternatives—will be taken up in greater detail below. In the cases already cited it is clear that coercion has a profound effect on freedom. It is the connection between coercion, freedom, and individual rights which will provide the basis in later chapters for an account of the justification of coercion.

The victim of coercion differs from a person in normal circumstances in that the coercer has detached the victim's actions and their consequences from his choices and desires. The victim of coercion cannot choose freely: he can choose only between the alternatives of complying with the threat and risking the threatened penalty. The moral presumption against coercion arises from this dissociation of action and outcome from choice. Coercion, it will be argued, infringes on the victim's freedom and violates his rights. It is justifiable only when other moral considerations outweigh these objections.

Coercion, Compulsion, and Duress

There are several ways involving force or deprivation of freedom in which one person can influence another's action. In the first place, a person may be *physically compelled*. A person may be forced to drop a gun, for example, when another pries his fingers open. Or a person may be forced to press the button which releases a canister of laughing gas into the White House air conditioning system when another person seizes her hand, places it over the button, and applies pressure to her arm.

Suppose that, in the latter case, someone asks, "Who pressed the button?" We might reply, "Ellen did." Such an answer would be true, as far as it goes, but it would be misleading to omit any mention of the circumstances of her act. Indeed, it would be more appropriate to name the person who held her finger to the button instead in response to such a question. For an act which results from physical force of this kind is not really the victim's act at all. The victim has not even a restricted freedom of action. She is unable to act otherwise than as she does, and her action—if we may speak of it as *her* action at all—is in no sense voluntary. The victim does not act but is the instrument by which another acts. If a burglar picks me up and uses my head to batter down a door, I am no more accountable for breaking and entering than I would be if he had used my hammer.

Cases such as those I have described have been classified by some writers as instances of one kind of coercion. Harry Frankfurt, for example, distinguishes "physical coercion" from other kinds of coercion.[1] But to call such cases coercive seems to extend the term beyond its usual use. Coercion is a way of causing a person to choose a certain action from among a restricted set of alternatives, and it essentially involves the victim's intentional action. For that reason it seems more accurate to distinguish *physical compulsion*, as I shall refer to cases such as those mentioned above, from coercion.

Coercion in its proper sense may or may not involve the application of physical force; what is essential is the imposition of a threat of force or harm. A person may be coerced to give up his money at gunpoint, or he may be coerced to reveal a secret by a threat to disclose damaging information about him. A coerced act is an intentional act: it is an act which the victim of coercion chooses to perform, given the choice between it and the threatened penalty. Yet it is not an act chosen freely, since the coercer has imposed on the victim a forced choice between an action which he may not want to do and a harm he does not want to suffer. The victim of coercion is clearly an agent, but his act is not voluntary in the same sense, or to the same degree, as an uncoerced act.

We may sum up the observations of the preceding paragraphs in a provisional definition of coercion:

(D1) A person P coerces another person Q to do (or to omit) an action A if and only if P employs the threat of force to bring it about that Q does (or omits) A.

This preliminary definition makes clear the difference between coercion and compulsion. Compulsion involves the use rather than the threat of force, and it does not cause the victim to act but makes him or her the instrument of another's action. Some of the examples already cited make it clear, however, that this definition will prove too narrow: for coercion need not involve the threat of force but may be accomplished through the threat of a highly undesirable but nonviolent penalty. This provisional definition will be amended below to take account of such cases.

In addition to distinguishing coercion from physical application of force, we also need to take note of the difference between coercion and a threat which interferes less severely with an agent's freedom. For not every threat is sufficient to coerce. The threat of any penalty for noncompliance alters the circumstances of action and may cause the person threatened to act differently than he would have had the threat not been made; but if the penalty is comparatively mild, it does not coerce the victim. "Throw a bomb in that classroom or I'll tell your wife about what you did at the party" is not a coercive threat; "Tell your wife or I'll bomb the schoolhouse," on the other hand, is very likely coercive. A person faced with a threat insufficient to coerce is acting under *duress:* his choice of actions and outcomes has been restricted by the threat attached to one action, but the threat does not coerce him to comply. He may reasonably choose to do the threatened action despite the threat and risk the penalty. In ordinary usage the scope of the term "duress" includes coercion as well; but we shall restrict the use of the term in this discussion to threats which are insufficient to coerce.

These, then, are the three ways in which one person may influence another's action: compulsion, coercion, and duress. In practice they may be difficult to distinguish precisely, and they may occur together. Torture, for example, involves the application of physical force but is also a means of coercion. It is not the actual force but the threat of continued suffering that compels a person being tortured to reveal a secret or confess to a crime. But it is also possible to employ the means of torture with no intent to coerce. Torture may be inflicted simply for the sake of the harm it does to its victim, without regard for her subsequent actions. In exceptional circumstances it might also amount to physical compulsion. An example will make clear how fine the line dividing various modes of influence can become: if a soldier is being tortured in order to force him to reveal a password, he may disclose it out of fear of further suffering—thus yielding to coercion—or he may be reduced to a semiconscious state in which he utters the password without realizing what he is saying—thereby suffering physical compulsion.[2]

Physical compulsion takes from the victim control over his actions. The person who imposes the compulsion assumes control over the victim's body and limbs. In the examples that have been cited, the victim of compulsion is used as the instrument of a particular action of the compeller. But compulsion may also be used to restrain a person from an act or a range of acts. A burglar may bind and gag his victim to prevent him from calling for help, for example, or a kidnapper may tie his victim to a tree to prevent him from escaping. Imprisonment is an instance of physical compulsion, together with certain legal deprivations. In a prison, however, the physical restraint of locked doors and barred windows is reinforced by coercive threats to deal harshly with attempts to escape.

In the case of coercion it is not the movement of the victim's body but—in a manner of speaking—the movement of his *will* that is subjected to the will of another. I will suggest below a way of making this claim more precise, but the contrast with compulsion and duress makes at least this much evident: a person coerced by the threat of serious harm can control his bodily movements in the normal way, but he must choose among a limited set of alternatives imposed on him by the coercer. He is not free to choose his actions and their outcome in the normal way, and in light of this lack of freedom the responsibility for his action, if he yields to the coercive threat, rests more with the coercer than with him. It is inappropriate to praise a person who donates his money to charity, or to blame another who spends his money foolishly, if he does so at gunpoint.

A person who acts under duress remains able to act as he chooses. His choice is restricted by the threat that is imposed, but the restriction is not as severe as in the case of coercion. It is insufficient to force him to act in a certain way. Neither his control over his body nor his will is subjugated to the will of the threatener.

It is part of the meaning of coercion, and not of duress, that the threat imposed *succeed* in affecting behavior. Coercion cannot be unsuccessful. To say this is not to say that coercive threats are irresistible. Perhaps there are some threats I cannot resist, as well as offers I cannot refuse; but a threat need not be one of these in order to be coercive. Rather, the concept of coercion includes success at affecting behavior. A threat, however dire, which fails to affect behavior is not a coercive threat after all but an unsuccessful attempt at coercion (and an instance of duress). We cannot define coercion, therefore, simply by referring to the kind or degree of threat. We must also know to whom the threat was made, what action was demanded, and how the person threatened acted subsequently.

The present chapter and the one which follows will be devoted to an exploration of precisely what it is that characterizes coercion. I will attempt to construct a definition which will help to identify coercion in the difficult borderline cases and which will also illuminate the characteristics of coercion in the clearest and most paradigmatic cases. As a way of drawing nearer our target, the remainder of the present chapter will examine a few representative accounts which other writers have offered of the nature of coercion. In the following chapter I will apply the insights gained from this brief review to the formulation of a definition which avoids some of the shortcoming of these other accounts.

Toward a Definition of Coercion

A representative definition of coercion is offered by Robert Dahl in the second edition of his text, *Modern Political Analysis*. In the context of a discussion of influence achieved through offers of rewards or threats of deprivation, Dahl states that coercion is "a particularly ominous kind of power" which "involves *only* the prospect of great loss." He explains:

> Suppose that A confronts B with the alternative "Your money or your life!" In general terms, B must choose between something bad or something very much worse. If B hands over his wallet, as he probably will, he may say later, "I had no choice." In one sense, of course, B does have a choice; but he has no reasonable or satisfactory choice. Hence he considers himself *coerced*. *Coercion*, then is a form of power that exists whenever A compels B to comply by confronting him *only* with alternatives involving severe deprivation.[3]

Dahl's account is an accurate description of some cases of coercion, but it is too restrictive. Although it is essential that the victim of coercion be brought to act by the threat of serious harm or loss, the action which the coercer demands need not involve any deprivation at all. If a highwayman threatens to kill me unless I sing the national anthem, I am coerced to sing—even if singing, far from being a serious harm, is one of my greatest pleasures. I may even thank the highwayman afterward for giving me an audience. As long as I sing out of fear of being killed, I am coerced none the less. Coercion is usually employed as a way of getting people to perform acts they would rather not do; but this is not essential to coercion, nor need the coerced action involve any loss or harm.

Dahl explicitly excludes from his account some cases which quite clearly fit his definition. He contrasts coercion, of which he takes robbery as a paradigm, with the legitimate demands of an organized government. But government, like the robber, offers individuals a

choice between two highly undesirable alternatives: pay taxes, for
example, or go to jail. According to the definition Dahl has given,
taxation is a clear instance of coercion.

Dahl is unwilling to recognize legal sanctions as coercive. To call the
legitimate exercise of power coercive, he says, "would run so contrary
to the usual meaning of language as to be confusing." Instead he
restricts the meaning of coercion: "Coercion implies *illegitimate* power
involving *only* the prospect of great loss."[4] Dahl's definition of coercion, however, as we have seen, includes no such requirement. Perhaps, then, we should take Dahl's assertion about the legitimacy of
coercion to be an additional element in his definition of coercion.
Illegitimacy, Dahl seems to be asserting, is a further necessary condition for power to be counted as coercive.

The implications of this position for political philosophy are important: by limiting the application of the term "coercive" to the illegitimate use of power Dahl takes coercion to be a morally evaluative
concept, a concept whose application entails a negative moral judgment. If he is correct in this, it follows that to identify a given action,
policy, or law as coercive is to judge it an illegitimate use of power.

Dahl is not alone in taking this view of the concept of coercion.
Economist Frank Knight, for example, writes in a discussion of the
nature of freedom:

> Scrutiny of any typical case of unfree behavior reveals that the
> coercive quality rests on an ethical condemnation, rather than the
> ethical condemnation on factually established unfreedom; or per-
> haps it is more accurate to say that they are merely different terms
> for the same thing. . . . We say that the victim of a highwayman is
> coerced, not because the character of his choice between the alter-
> natives presented is different from any other choice, but because we
> think the robber does "wrong" in making the alternatives what they
> are.
>
> . . . In no other sense is it possible to speak of coercion.[5]

In philosophical discussions of coercion other writers have asserted
that "compulsion is a moral notion"[6] and that "freedom is not a factual
issue per se but is rather an issue of the facts which are commonly said
to excuse. . . . Whether someone can sensibly be said to have a choice
must be a moral, not a factual, question."[7]

Shared by Dahl and the other writers quoted is the view that to
judge an action coercive is to make a negative moral judgment on the
act. "Coercion," according to this view, is not a morally neutral term
like "persuasion," or "delay," which leaves open the question of

whether in a particular instance it is right or justified. Rather, it is a morally condemnatory term like "seduction" or "evasion."

If this view is correct, any further investigation of the moral status of coercion seems rather futile, since the conclusion is foregone. But there are more weighty reasons for rejecting this view than the fact that it renders the remainder of this study superfluous. Although "coercion" is no doubt sometimes used in a morally condemnatory sense, it can also be used in a way which leaves the question of legitimacy open.

Coercion is a particular way of bringing a person to perform an action by means of a threat. Sometimes its use is justified, sometimes not. It is an interference with a person which *requires* justification; but such justification is not impossible. Further, I shall argue below, the requirement that coercion be morally defended—the presumption against coercion—need not be included as a defining condition of coercion, for it is a consequence of the way in which coercion affects the person.

The concept of coercion, I shall argue, is not an inherently condemnatory notion: coercion can be justified. But I do not intend to suggest that the concept of coercion has nothing at all to do with moral concepts. Although coercion is not a morally evaluative category, it is nevertheless a moral concept. For instances of coercion cannot be identified without relying on moral judgments. To say that an act constitutes coercion is to make certain implicit normative claims, not merely to assert descriptive facts. The nature of these normative claims will be spelled out as we proceed; the point I emphasize here is that to reject Dahl's claim does not entail a complete separation between coercion and moral concepts.

Doubtless the most meticulous and circuitous discussion of the conditions which constitute coercion is that offered by Robert Nozick in his article, "Coercion." The result of his multi-faceted and complex exploration of the varieties of coercion is the following compound definition:

A person P coerces a person Q into not doing an act A if and only if

1. P threatens to bring about or have brought about some consequence if Q does A (and knows he is threatening to do this);

2. A with this threatened consequence is rendered substantially less eligible as a course of action for Q than A was without this threatened consequence;

3. P makes this threat in order to get Q not to do A, intending that Q realize that he's been threatened by P;

4. Q does not do A;

5. Part of Q's reason for not doing A is to avoid (or lessen the likelihood of) the consequence which P has threatened to bring about or have brought about; and

6. Q knows that P has threatened to do the something mentioned in (1) if he, Q, does A.[8]

As stated, these are conditions under which a person is coerced to refrain from an action; they may be revised in obvious ways to apply to coercion to perform an action.

Nozick's definition remedies the defects of Dahl's. It does not require that the coercer force the victim to choose between two highly undesirable options but only that the coercer render some course of action much less attractive than it would otherwise be. Nozick's condition (4) recognizes that coercion is exercised only when it is successfully exercised, i. e., only when the victim actually complies with the threat. It is impossible for the coercion to fail in its effect, since an attempt at coercion which fails to influence the action of the victim is not coercive after all.

I have quoted above Nozick's initial version of (3), but this is a version which he eventually rejects as too restrictive. In the first place, it is possible that the coercer may be indifferent to whether the victim will comply with his demand or suffer the threatened consequence. Nozick offers as an example a social scientist who is studying the reaction of randomly chosen subjects to the threat, "Your money or your life," and is authorized to kill anyone who fails to hand over his money. Such a researcher is interested only in the outcome of his survey, and he will be disappointed—as a scientist—if all of the subjects in his "sample" comply with his threat; and so condition (3) is not satisfied. We need not appeal to such farfetched and barbarous examples to cast doubt on (3): there are no doubt ordinary highwaymen, and for that matter police officers, who would be quite as happy if their victims refused to comply with their threats and suffered the consequences as if they complied. It is essential to coercion that the threatened penalty be very much worse than the act demanded, but whether the coercer prefers one outcome over the other is unimportant.

In the second place, the person who makes the threat may be bluffing and have no intention of carrying out his threat, and the victim may be coerced all the same. (The social scientist would fall into this category if he did not intend to kill noncomplying subjects.) In order to accommodate these two sorts of cases Nozick substitutes a more complicated disjunction for (3):

3'. (Part of) P's reason for deciding to bring about this consequence or have it brought about, if Q does A, is that P believes this consequence worsens Q's alternative of doing A (i. e., that P believes that this consequence worsens Q's alternative of doing A, or that Q would believe it does). If P has not decided to bring about the consequence, then (part of) P's reason for saying he will bring about the consequence, or have it brought about, if Q does A is that (P believes) Q will believe this consequence worsens Q's alternative of doing A.[9]

Nozick also adds a final condition: that the consequence be such that, in P's view, Q will be worse off having done A and suffered the consequence than if he did not do A and P did not bring about the consequence. This is introduced to exclude cases in which the consequence P intends to bring about simply nullifies Q's action. "If you say another word I shall turn off my hearing aid," Nozick believes, is not a coercive threat.[10]

Despite the care with which Nozick has formulated his definition and the complexities with which it bristles, his account has a serious flaw. The conditions which Nozick enumerates may be necessary for coercion, but they are not sufficient.

The principal defect of Nozick's account is this: according to the definition he has given, a person may be coerced into any sort of action (or omission to act) by the threat of any undesirable consequence. All that is required is that the alternative that the coercer wishes to prevent the victim from choosing be attached to a consequence which renders it substantially less eligible. Nozick therefore fails to distinguish coercion from duress.

Any action is rendered substantially less eligible if it is attached to the loss of a hundred dollars. But if a person tells me, "Unless you help me pull off a bank job next week I will not repay the hundred dollars I owe you," he does not coerce me into helping him. Nor does he coerce me if, for example, he threatens to destroy something valuable that I own. The loss threatened may be substantial—thus meeting clause (2) of Nozick's definition—and yet insufficient to coerce. Particular circumstances might make such a threat coercive, however: to a person in dire need the loss of one hundred dollars might be a coercive threat.

If a threat involves physical violence, the situation is more complicated, and we must take into account not only the seriousness of the threat but also the nature of the action (or omission) which the threatener demands. If Paula threatens to beat Quincy up unless he gives her a dollar, he may properly claim to be coerced. But if Paula threatens him with a beating unless he kills someone whom she dislikes, Quincy cannot offer the same excuse if he complies. The threat of a broken toe is probably sufficient to coerce someone to make an illegal U-turn—but not sufficient to coerce him to commit arson.

Whether a threat is sufficient to coerce depends not only on the conditions which Nozick has enumerated but also on the *character of the act demanded* by the coercer and on the *nature of the harm* involved. A threat which is insufficient to coerce nevertheless influences the threatened person's choice of action and limits his freedom, but it does not interfere as severely as does a coercive threat.

Nozick, it should be noted, suggests that we may need the notion of a lessened degree of coercion. But he sees the need for such a concept only in cases where a threat is only part of a person's reason for acting as he does. "In cases where Q's whole reason for not doing A is to avoid or lessen the likelihood of P's threatened consequences . . . P coerces Q into not doing A," Nozick states.[11] But whether a person is actually coerced depends not only on whether other motives besides the threat influence his decision but also on the character of the threat and of the act and on the circumstances under which the threat is made.

Despite this important omission, Nozick's account of coercion is in other respects sound. He recognizes that coercion cannot be unsuccessful, since his condition (4) states that the victim of coercion must have acted in the way the coercer demanded. Nozick also correctly requires, in his condition (3) (and also, less obviously, in the revised [3']) that coercion be intentional. The coercer must know that he is threatening his victim and must intend to influence his behavior by doing so. The other parts of Nozick's definition specify exactly what is meant by influencing another's behavior with a threat. The definition I propose below will draw a clear distinction, as Nozick does not, between coercion and duress, but it will presuppose the correctness of much of what Nozick says about the character and function of coercive and other threats.

What Makes a Threat Coercive?

Is it possible to coerce a person by threatening the loss of a sum of money? If so, how large a sum is sufficient to coerce? A hundred dollars? A thousand? A week's earnings?

These questions cannot be answered with a simple "yes" or "no." Whether a threat is coercive depends not only on the amount of loss threatened but also on the victim's circumstances—on how much the loss means to him. The threat of a loss of a hundred dollars is a grave threat to a starving and penniless man but not to John Paul Getty. The victim's circumstances may thus make the difference between a coercive and a noncoercive threat. The threat of tickling is not normally coercive, but perhaps it might be so—if the threat were made, for example, to the pilot of an airliner on a landing approach.

It is impossible to draw up a list of which threats are coercive threats, therefore; for a threat which is sufficient to coerce one person under certain circumstances may be insufficient to coerce another or to coerce the same person under different circumstances. If I am accosted by a man on the street who threatens to beat me up unless I give him my watch, I may legitimately claim to be coerced to comply. But a heavyweight prizefighter would not be coerced. The difference between our situations can be described by saying that the fighter has a choice, where I do not: if I try to overpower the thief, I am likely to be injured, but the fighter can expect to deliver rather than receive a beating. But if the fighter's situation were different—if the thief were armed, or if the fighter had a broken arm—he too would be coerced. If, on the other hand, the act demanded by the threatener were a grave moral wrong—if he threatened a beating unless I planted a bomb in a school bus, for example—then, however weak or strong I may be, I cannot claim to be coerced.

Before trying to sort out difficult cases, we should take note of a few central and relatively obvious facts about coercion. First, some severe threats are sufficient to coerce nearly anyone to do nearly anything. A loaded pistol or a sharpened knife will persuade anyone except a fool or a hero to give up his money, fly his airplane to Havana, or sign a false confession.

But, second, even such a threat will not coerce everyone—for there are heroes as well as fools who defy even threats such as these. It follows that no threat, however serious, is intrinsically or inevitably coercive.

Third, the qualification we included a moment ago—"sufficient to coerce nearly anyone *to do nearly anything*"—is essential. For there are some acts which cannot be coerced. One cannot be coerced to kill someone deliberately, for example, for even the threat of immediate death is not sufficient to constitute coercion to commit murder.

The third claim, perhaps, is a matter of controversy: some would argue that a person can be coerced to kill. But a careful assessment of the nature of coercive threats shows that this is impossible. To assert that I have been coerced to act is to assert that I had effectively no choice but to comply, that I could not reasonably have acted otherwise. But even when threatened with death unless I kill someone I have a choice: I am able, and indeed ought, to risk being killed (if I cannot escape or overpower the threatener) rather than kill another person. To say that I was coerced to kill in such a case is to imply the false claim that I had no reasonable choice but to act as I did.

There are two distinct kinds of relativity, as the examples we have just examined suggest, which are relevant to the question of whether a particular threat is coercive. First, coerciveness is relative both to the *person* to whom the threat is made and to the *circumstances* of the threat. The threat of a beating, for example, is more likely to coerce a ninety-five-pound weakling than a prizefighter. The threat of a broken finger is a serious threat to anyone but far more so to a concert pianist. Just how serious a threat is depends on both the character and the situation of the person threatened.

Second, coerciveness is relative to the *nature of the act* demanded by the coercer. The threat of a broken finger may coerce someone to refuse to cooperate with the police, but it cannot coerce anyone to commit murder. The second kind of relativity, it may be noted, draws our attention to an element of moral judgment which is involved in the very concept of coercion. The reason why no one can be coerced to commit murder is that murder is a serious moral wrong, whatever the motive or provocation. In order to classify threats as coercive or noncoercive, therefore, we must judge the morality or immorality of overt actions.[12]

Both of these kinds of relativity involve subjective as well as objective elements. The relativity to individual and to circumstance depends not merely on the victim's physical strength and the probability that the threat will be carried out but also on how the threat and the circumstances in which it is made affect that individual. The threat of being tickled is inconsequential to a person who is insensitive or moderately sensitive to tickling, but it might coerce a person who is so sensitive as to be paralyzed by tickling. Threatening to release a swarm of bees would be a moderately serious threat to most people but an extremely serious one to a person with a strong allergic reaction to insect stings. Similarly, the relativity to the seriousness of the act must be determined by the seriousness of the act for the particular individual involved. A threat which would coerce an American farmer to kill a cow would not be sufficient to coerce a Hindu.

There are two senses in which a threat may be "insufficient to coerce." In the first place, a threat may simply not be severe enough to achieve its purpose. Fines for overtime parking have an effect on behavior, but because the cost involved is, for most people, an annoyance rather than a significant loss, such fines should not be considered coercive. (They do take place against a coercive background, however, since there is an implicit threat of more severe sanctions if they are not paid.) The severity of the threat may hinge on particular circumstances: if I have a Hindu employee and threaten to withhold his wages unless he butchers a cow for me, he is likely to accept the loss rather than violate a religious obligation. My threat will very likely fail because it is insufficient to coerce.

There is another way in which a threat may fail to coerce, even if it actually leads to the action which the coercer demands: if the threat is not severe enough to leave the victim only one reasonable choice, then, whatever the victim's subsequent action, she has not been coerced. And the victim's own testimony about the severity of a threat is not determinative of whether coercion has occurred, for an individual's claim that she had no choice but to submit to a threat may be false. A person threatened with financial loss unless she injures a child is unlikely to comply with the threat; but even if she does, claiming to be coerced, coercion has not occurred. Such a threat is insufficient to coerce such an action and constitutes instead a relatively mild case of duress.

Judgments of the severity of a threat are by no means purely subjective, however. An individual's perception of the situation is not the decisive test of coercion. Someone who claims to have been co-erced to kill his mother by the threat of being tickled is simply wrong: no matter how greatly he may have feared the threatened outcome, he was not coerced. What seems to be required is an *objective* assessment of the *subjective* severity of the threat, first in relation to person and circumstance and then in relation to act.

Thus a person with an allergy to bee stings will properly count the threat of a sting as a serious threat, more serious than it would be for a normal person. Killing a cow is a far more serious wrong to a Hindu than to a Baptist. But in neither case is the individual's subjective assessment the sole determinant of the severity of the threat. The severity of a threat is relative to the person threatened and his circum-stances, and its coerciveness depends on whether the victim takes the act demanded to be a serious wrong; yet these judgments must be based not simply on the individual's reported perceptions of the threat and the act but on conditions which can be observed, and whose effects can be taken into account, by others.

Factors which increase the severity of threats include more than purely physical conditions, and a person's claim to feel overcome by fright may be grounded in a known and observed psychological con-dition. Someone who knows her victim's phobias may exploit her knowledge by coercing him with threats which would only constitute moderate duress to another person. Conversely, the seriousness of a threat is not increased by the victim's unusual physical sensitivity unless the victim knows about his condition.

Even in the case of phobias there is an objective element. If the coerciveness of a threat is called into question—if coercion is offered, for example, as a legal defense—we are entitled to demand evidence that the individual actually suffers from such an abormally strong fear, evidence which may be drawn from his behavior on other occasions. The victim's claim that he was coerced does not settle the issue.

It is not precisely an individual's unusual *fear* which makes a threat more serious in the presence of a neurotic fear of insects but rather the greater than normal *harm* which is inflicted on such a person by unleashing a swarm of bees on him. Psychological harm is no less real than physical harm, and the terror which a person with an abnormal fear of insects feels in the presence of bees is a serious harm, more serious than the harm which the same circumstances would cause a normal person.

In an extreme case of pathological fear, a person may be altogether unable to put aside his fear and defy the threat. It may be beyond the victim's power to undertake an action which exposes him to the object of his fear. This possibility might appear to provide a counterexample to the claim that some actions, such as murder, cannot be coerced, for a coercer who exploits such a weakness may create a situation in which the victim has no choice but to do whatever the coercer demands. Whether in fact such cases occur is a thorny question of motivational psychology. But it is clear that, if there are any such cases, they resemble physical compulsion more closely than coercion.

Just how severe need a threat be in order to be a coercive threat? The distinction mentioned above between relativity to the agent and relativity to the act suggests two alternative ways of answering this question. First, it might be said that a coercive threat is a threat so strong that the victim *cannot* resist it. Given the victim's character and circumstances, he cannot but comply with the threat. The coerciveness of the threat, on this account, is determined primarily by the first kind of relativity mentioned above—relativity to the person coerced and to his circumstances. Or, second, it might be said that a coercive threat is one which is sufficiently strong to *justify* the victim in complying with it. On this account, the more important relativity is to the act demanded.

The first of these criteria for coerciveness is unsatisfactory, for it fails to identify coercive threats correctly. Whether the victim could resist the threat does not determine whether he is coerced. In the first place, if a deterministic theory of human action is correct, then every act is such that the agent could not do otherwise, and it would appear that every threat which succeeds in affecting another's action is a coercive threat. But the category of coercion would then become far too inclusive: parking fines, library overdue charges, and the rules of public swimming pools, all of which involve very minor penalties and yet usually succeed in shaping behavior, would be labelled coercive.

But let us suppose that the actions in question are not determined, or that we can offer a satisfactory account of what it means to say that a person is able to do otherwise even when his action is in some sense determined. Even so, the first account of coercion is unacceptable. For on many occasions a genuinely coercive threat is one which the victim could have resisted. If a person reveals a secret rather than be severely beaten, it does not matter whether he could have chosen to undergo the beating. The threat is a coercive threat regardless of whether the individual could have defied it. Perhaps he could have, perhaps he could not; what is essential is that the threat was so severe that he had no reasonable choice but to submit.

The second alternative, I believe, points the way toward a correct account of the difference between coercive and noncoercive threats: coercive threats are sufficiently serious to justify the victim in complying with them. Coerciveness is determined, then, above all by the relation between the threat and the act demanded, though this relativity is in turn influenced by the character and circumstances of the victim. A threat which is sufficient to coerce one person into singing "The Star-Spangled Banner" may be insufficient, for example, to coerce an anti-American activist or monk under a vow of silence to do the same. A less serious threat might coerce a passing motorist to drive a terrorist to his destination than would be required to coerce a military guard, who is under a special role-based obligation not to leave his post, to do so.

The first criterion suggested above, that a coercive threat is one which is so strong that the victim cannot resist it, treats coercion as an *excuse*, like physical compulsion. Coercion, however, is more than an excuse: a person who claims to have been coerced claims to have acted in the only reasonable way, not necessarily in the only possible way. Coercion is not simply an excuse but a *justification*, similar in this respect to self-defense as a justification for having injured someone. The second criterion correctly includes this moral element.

To sum up the discussion of the last few pages, the distinction between coercion and duress—the distinction which is missing from Nozick's account—is based chiefly on how important the threatened loss is and on how seriously objectionable the act demanded is. We might say loosely that when a person acts because of a threat, he has been coerced if the threat is bad enough and the act he does is not too bad.

Discrimination among coercion, attempted coercion, and alleged coercion may involve a judgment of character similar to that which is at issue in cases of weakness of will.[13] A threat is likely to coerce when a person with the normal stock of fortitude and of moral scruples would comply rather than defy the threat and would judge that he had no other reasonable choice. A cowardly person may be coerced by a lesser threat, if the penalty is one which he cannot bring himself to risk. The fact that, in the same circumstances, a more courageous person would not have been coerced does not entail that he was not coerced. A person who is coerced because of his own lack of courage is genuinely coerced, and he cannot be held responsible in the full sense for his act—although we might hold him responsible, and blame him, for not having developed a more robust will. The threat justifies the act, even though the agent's susceptibility to threats may be a moral fault. All the same, there are some acts—murder, for example—which no degree of faint-heartedness can excuse on grounds of coercion.

How difficult a person is to coerce, then, is a measure of his courage. It would appear also to be a measure of his moral character: a person with few moral scruples would mistakenly judge that, say, beating a stranger is not such a bad thing to do, and he might claim— falsely—that a threat to take a thousand dollars from him was sufficient to coerce him to do such an act. It is more accurate, however, to describe this as a case of noncoercive duress—duress which the person ought to have resisted but which because of his bad moral character he did not.

Duress and Coercion: Two Accounts

Nozick's account of coercion, I have argued, needs to be supplemented by a clearer account of the difference between coercion and duress. For assistance in stating this distinction precisely, I turn to two other recent accounts of the concept of coercion: that offered by Bernard Gert and that stated independently by Harry Frankfurt and by Gerald Dworkin. Gert offers an account of coercion which includes the distinction missing from Nozick's account in an article on "Coercion and Freedom."[14] I shall state his view briefly without attempting to summarize the metaethical structure in which it is embedded.

A necessary condition of acting either freely or under coercion,

Gert states, is having the ability to will what one does. A person has the ability to will to do an action of a certain kind if and only if there are reasonable incentives which would lead her to do it and reasonable incentives which would lead her not to do it. But some incentives are unreasonable: they are incentives such that it would be unreasonable to expect any rational person faced with such incentives not to act on them. Threats of harm may be unreasonable incentives. When a person acts as she does because of a threat which constitutes an unreasonable incentive, she is coerced to do as she does. Her action is voluntary, since it is the kind of action which she has the ability to will, and yet it is unfree.[15]

According to this account, whether a person who submits to a threat acts under coercion depends both on the character of the acts she performs and on the threatened penalty if she does not—and these are precisely the elements that were missing from Nozick's account. If the threat and the action to which it is attached are such that it would be unreasonable to expect a rational person to defy the threat, then one who complies with the threat is acting under coercion—even though it is possible that she might, however unreasonably, have defied the threat. Threats which do not meet this standard, however, are not coercive. Threatened with a broken thumb unless she kills someone, a rational person is expected to defy the threat and bear the penalty. Therefore someone who complies with such a threat cannot claim to be coerced. Gert's account, unlike Nozick's, includes a clear distinction between coercive and noncoercive threats.

The principal shortcoming of Gert's account is that it does not tell us very much. Gert provides a framework within which we may identify coercive threats, viz. according to what it would be reasonable to expect a rational person to do under similar circumstances. This standard offers a way to restate our intuitions about when a person is coerced, but it does not seem helpful for resolving difficult cases.

Moreover, to invoke as the criterion of coercion a rational person's assessment of a situation is misleading. Reference to what a rational agent would do is sometimes a useful device in ethics. Its function is to exclude certain sorts of extraneous and irrelevant influences on a judgment or decision, and its usefulness is greatest when the extraneous factors can be identified precisely. But it is not at all clear what influences are extraneous to determination of whether a threat is coercive or what kinds of reasons would motivate a rational agent. Would a rational person be moved by fear of injury or death? How strong would his fear be? Would he make an objective appraisal of the pain threatened, discounted by the credibility of the threat, without being moved by fear? Or, on the other hand, would he consider only the rightness or wrongness of the alternative actions open to him? But how are rightness and wrongness to be determined?

Gert offers a highly rationalistic account of what constitute good and evil: a good is that which no rational person will avoid for himself unless he has a reason, an evil that which no rational person will seek for himself unless he has a reason.[16] We cannot appeal to this definition to determine how the rational person would act, for to do so would lead us into a circle.

More important, the standard of a rational person's action—even if it were clear just what this standard amounts to—cannot be determinative of what threats are coercive; for such a standard takes no account of the subjective aspects of coercion mentioned above. A rational person would presumably be free from exceptionally strong or neurotic fears. But a flesh-and-blood human being may be coerced by a threat which plays on his particular sensitivities and fears, even if the threat would be of little consequence to an ideally rational agent.

Human beings are not purely rational agents. If they were, coercion would occur much less frequently than it does. Reference to the standard of rational action cannot supply a satisfactory criterion for identifying coercive threats.

A different way of isolating coercion from lesser degrees of duress is taken by Gerald Dworkin and by Frankfurt.[17] Specific to coercion, they suggest, are two features: First, the person coerced has no choice but to submit because he is moved by motives which he cannot control. Second, the victim is compelled to act from a motive which he would rather not act from. Thus Frankfurt:

> It [coercion] requires that the victim of a threat should have no alternative to submission. . . .
>
> This requirement can only be satisfied when the threat appeals to desires or motives which are beyond the victim's ability to control, or when the victim is convinced that this is the case. If the victim's desire or motive to avoid the penalty with which he is threatened is—or is taken by him to be—so powerful that he cannot prevent it from leading him to submit to the threat, then he really has no alternative other than to submit. He cannot effectively choose to do otherwise. It is only then that it *may* be proper to regard him as bearing no moral responsibility for his submission. Whether or not it *is* in fact proper to regard him so—i.e., as being genuinely coerced—depends on whether a still further condition . . . is also satisfied.

That condition, which Frankfurt states in essentially the same terms Dworkin had earlier used, is that

> . . . coercion must involve a violation of the victim's autonomy. The victim of coercion is necessarily either moved in some way against his will or his will is in some way circumvented.

And the interference with the victim's will which is a necessary condition for coercion occurs when the victim

> is moved into compliance by a desire which is not only irresistible but which he would overcome if he could.

This condition, according to Frankfurt, holds of some irresistible offers and of all irresistible threats.

> In submitting to a threat, a person invariably does something which he does not really want to do. Hence irresistible threats, unlike irresistible offers, are necessarily coercive.[18]

Frankfurt and Dworkin are correct, I believe, in linking coercion closely with questions of autonomy and in asserting that coercion subverts or disables the will. But the first of the two conditions which they enumerate is difficult to articulate precisely. Moreover, if I understand the two conditions correctly, neither is in fact necessary for coercion.

Before examining these conditions more closely, however, we should note a surprising consequence of Frankfurt's definition, one which he acknowledges at the end of his article: coercion does not require the intervention of another person. The two conditions may be satisfied regardless of whether one's actions are constrained by another's threat or by conditions which occur independently of anyone's actions or intentions. My choice of which path to take is equally coerced, according to Frankfurt's account, whether another person threatens to start an avalanche that will kill me if I walk on the left-hand path or merely warns me that my walking on the path will trigger an avalanche.

Frankfurt takes this as a curious fact about coercion. I believe it is rather a curious feature of Frankfurt's account of coercion—a feature in light of which his definition includes far more than we usually include in the concept. In the remainder of this discussion I follow Nozick rather than Frankfurt and include as essential to coercion the actions and intentions of the coercer. To speak of being coerced by an avalanche or an automobile breakdown, if we can speak in this way at all, is a metaphorical use of the term "coercion."

This restriction is not an arbitrary definitional fiat. Coercion is a way of influencing behavior, and our interest in coercion is principally an interest in understanding and assessing this means of interpersonal influence. At least insofar as it is a concern of moral and political philosophy, coercion is an act of one person over against another. We want to know whether a certain action is coerced because we want to identify and assess the relationship between the persons involved.

Let us return now to the two conditions which Frankfurt believes are necessary for coercion and examine them in turn. The first is that the victim have no choice but to submit, in the sense that the threat appeals to motives so powerful that he cannot but comply.

This requirement, it has been argued above, is mistaken: coercion, unlike compulsion, does not render it impossible for the victim to do otherwise than as he does.[19] What is distinctive of coercion is that the victim is threatened with a penalty sufficiently severe, in light of the act demanded, to justify him in submitting. Perhaps he is able to defy the threat and risk the consequences, perhaps not. This is unimportant, and inessential to coercion. What is essential is not the victim's inability to defy the threat but rather the unacceptable cost of doing so.

Frankfurt's second condition is that coercion must interfere with the victim's will in that the victim of coercion must be moved to act by motives which he would prefer not to be moved by. There is an ambiguity in this assertion which hinges on how broadly or how narrowly we construe the victim's motive for action. On either reading, however, this condition also appears to be mistaken.

The motive which moves the victim of coercion is usually fear—fear of the harm which the coercer has threatened. It is true in general that we would prefer not to have to do things out of fear of harm. We would rather make up our own minds about what to do and what not to do than have to act under threat. Nevertheless we cannot infer from this fact that, when circumstances warrant fear, we would prefer not to act from fear. On the contrary, to be entirely free from the restraining influence of fear would be to live not just dangerously but foolishly: we know that we cannot always arrive at an accurate and dispassionate estimate of all of the risks we face, and the emotional response of fear is a useful if inaccurate indicator of risk. Fear is an emotion which we normally prefer not to experience. But as a motive for action, when it is appropriate and not unfounded or exaggerated, it restrains us from actions which would cause us harm.

The person to whom a threat is made would normally rather not *have* to act out of fear, in the sense that he would rather the threat had not been made (though I shall suggest below that this need not be the case). Nevertheless, once the threat has been made, he may *want* to act out of fear. This does not—as Frankfurt's definition implies—make him any the less coerced. Or, on the other hand, he may want not to act out of fear. He may wish, even as he submits to the threat, that he were able to put it out of his mind and act as if he had not been threatened. But whether he wishes he were not acting from fear has no bearing on the question of whether he is coerced. One person may act from fear which he willingly accepts as a motive for action and yet be coerced; another may act from fear which he wants not to act from and yet act under duress rather than coercion, if the threat is a relatively mild one.

Frankfurt's basic mistake, I believe, is to assume that fear, or some other emotional and nonrational response, is essential to coercion. This assumption is unsound. Although fear usually motivates coerced acts, this need not be so. A person may comply with a threat as a result of a rational assessment of the threatened penalty, the credibility of the threat, and the undesirability of the act demanded. The victim of coercion in such a case acts in order to avoid or minimize harm, and his motive is one which we want to be moved by.

Frankfurt's assumption appears initially plausible because cases such as this are, after all, unusual. Normally we prefer not to be placed in situations where we must act in response to a threat. There are cases, we have noted, in which we respond to threats rationally and unemotionally; and yet we do not normally want to be threatened in the first place. But there are exceptions even to this generalization. A kleptomaniac who wishes he would not steal might be happy to be threatened by a store detective with harsh treatment, since fear of the penalty will enable him to overcome his impulse to steal. A person who wants to stop smoking cigarettes, all else having failed, might ask a friend to use whatever force is necessary to prevent him from lighting up whenever he begins looking for a cigarette.[20] In such cases the individual recognizes that his short-term desires and impulses are inconsistent with his long-term desires, and he therefore wants in certain circumstances to be compelled to act out of fear of harm. On each particular occasion in which the individual is moved to act by fear of threatened consequences, he is coerced to act as he would, on balance and in the long run, prefer to act.

The motivational character of coercion, therefore, seems to be misrepresented by Frankfurt's account. On this point Nozick, too, misunderstands the nature of threats, for he argues that the nonvoluntary character of a choice made under threat is grounded in the fact that a rational agent would always prefer not to be placed in a threat situation than to be placed in the same situation without the threat.[21] But situations such as those just mentioned show that this condition, whether or not it is true of ideally rational agents, is not true of ordinary persons.[22] We all make some choices which we later, or even at the time of choosing, recognize to be inconsistent with our long-term principles, desires, and interests.[23] In some of these situations, given the choice, we would rather be compelled by a threat to make the better choice than make the worse choice freely. Describing coercion from the point of view of a hypothetical rational agent obscures this fact from Nozick's view, as it had excluded from Gert's account the important nonrational determinants of coercion.

There are some circumstances, therefore, in which we want to be coerced. Sometimes we want to be motivated by fear of undesirable consequences. Such situations make it evident that we cannot define coercion—as Nozick, Gert, and Frankfurt have done—by reference to the operation of unwanted motives. Coercion does not occur only when a person is moved by a motive by which he would prefer not to be moved.[24]

It is not necessary to coercion that one act out of undesired motives. Frankfurt's account of the relation between coercion and the will, therefore, rests on a false assumption. His account leads us in the right direction, however, by focusing on the fact that coercion involves an interference with the victim's will. In the following chapter a definition of coercion will be offered which, I believe, will avoid the pitfalls of those which we have surveyed so far. And, having offered a definition, we will go on in subsequent chapters to explore in greater detail the ways in which the will of the victim is affected by coercive threats.

Notes

1. Harry Frankfurt, "Coercion and Moral Responsibility," in Ted Honderich, ed., *Essays on Freedom of Action* (Boston: Routledge and Kegan Paul, 1973), 66. Frankfurt does not have a label for the more usual cases of coercion through threats. Michael Bayles suggests the terms "operational" and "dispositional" coercion for what I refer to above as physical compulsion and coercion, respectively; see "A Concept of Coercion," in *Coercion, Nomos*, vol. 14, ed. J. Roland Pennock and John W. Chapman (Chicago: Aldine Atherton Co., 1972), 17.

2. The example is from Frankfurt, "Coercion and Moral Responsibility," 65–66.

3. Robert Dahl, *Modern Political Analysis*, 2d ed. (Englewood Cliff., N.J.: Prentice-Hall, 1970), 33. This account of coercion does not occur in the otherwise similar discussion of power in the first edition of the book.

4. Dahl, *Modern Political Analysis*, 33–34; italics his.

5. Frank Knight, "Freedom as Fact and Criterion," in *Freedom and Reform: Essays in Economics and Social Philosophy* (New York: Harper Brothers, 1974), 10, 12.

6. Austin Duncan-Jones, "Freedom to Do Otherwise," *Cambridge Journal* 3, no. 12 (September 1950): 753.

7. Richard N. Bronaugh, "Freedom as the Absence of an Excuse," *Ethics* 74, no. 3 (April 1964): 163. This and the previous references are cited by Gerald Dworkin, who undertakes to

refute their common claim in "Compulsion and Moral Concepts," *Ethics* 78, no. 3 (April 1968): 227–33.

8. Robert Nozick, "Coercion," in Sidney Morgenbesser, Patrick Suppes, and Morton White, eds., *Philosophy, Science, and Method: Essays in Honor of Ernest Nagel* (New York: St. Martin's Press, 1969), 440–45.

9. Nozick, "Coercion," 442–43.

10. Nozick, "Coercion," 443.

11. Nozick, "Coercion," 464.

12. The distinction between these two kinds of relativity was pointed out to me by T. M. Scanlon, whose comments have also been very helpful in formulating the account given below of how serious a threat must be in order to be coercive.

13. See Donald Davidson, "How Is Weakness of Will Possible?", in Joel Feinberg, ed., *Moral Concepts* (Oxford: Oxford University Press, 1969), 93–113.

14. Bernard Gert, "Coercion and Freedom," in *Coercion, Nomos*, vol. 14, 30–48.

15. Gert, "Coercion and Freedom," 31–32, 34. Gert states that offers of benefits are never unreasonable incentives and hence cannot coerce. This issue is discussed further in Chapter 3, below.

16. Gert, "Coercion and Freedom," 33. See also his book, *The Moral Rules* (New York: Harper and Row, 1973), esp. chap. 3.

17. Frankfurt, "Coercion and Moral Responsibility," 75–84; Gerald Dworkin, "Acting Freely," *Nous* 4, no. 4 (November 1970): 367–83.

18. Frankfurt, "Coercion and Moral Responsibility," 77–78, 80, 81. Dworkin's account of coercion is similar to Frankfurt's but emphasizes the undesired desires which operate, and he does not state as strongly as does Frankfurt the necessity of absence of choice. His account is also directed more toward conditions for being free and acting freely than toward conditions for being coerced.

19. One can imagine circumstances in which to do otherwise would be impossible: suppose the coercer implants electrodes in the victim's brain and stimulates them in such a way as to cause him to perform a certain act. Or suppose he persuades the victim that he is going to hypnotize him for therapeutic purposes and, while the victim is under hypnosis, instructs him to do a certain act. These, however, are not really cases of coercion but sophisticated forms of physical compulsion.

20. Compare the related argument of J. Howard Sobel in "The Need for Coercion," in *Coercion, Nomos*, vol. 14, 148–177, that even hyperrational act-utilitarians might be unable to pursue the best course of action in certain circumstances, or even to act at all, without coercive measures of enforcement.

21. Nozick, "Coercion," pp. 458–464.

22. Cf. Virginia Held, "Coercion and Coercive Offers," in *Coercion, Nomos*, vol. 14, 54–55.

23. On this point cf. Davidson, "How Is Weakness of Will Possible?"

24. In a more recent article, a response to an article by Don Locke on the topic, "Three Concepts of Free Action," published in *The Aristotelian Society Supplement* 49 (1975): 113–125, Frankfurt revises his earlier account of coercion. Here he distinguishes three situations: those of Type A, in which a person must choose an action from among alternatives all of which are in some measure undesirable; those of Type B, in which a person is moved to act by a motive which he would prefer not to be moved by; and those of Type C, in which a person is moved by an irresistible desire without attempting to prevent that desire from moving him. Only situations of Type C constitute coercion, according to Frankfurt's revised account; he no longer requires that the motive which causes a person to submit to coercion be in disharmony with his other desires. In effect Frankfurt has here discarded his second criterion for coercion and placed the entire emphasis on what was in the earlier article his first condition. The objection above to that condition—viz., that persons who are coerced need not be moved irresistibly to act as they do—retains its force against his revised account.

3
COERCION DEFINED

It is a dark and stormy night. Quentin is walking down the street when Pamela jumps out from behind a Good Humor truck, points a revolver at him, and exclaims, "Your money or your life!"

What can happen, once such a threat has been made? If we disregard the possibility of interference by others (the street is otherwise deserted, and if there is a driver in the Good Humor truck, he is deaf), one of the following six outcomes may occur:

1. Quentin hands over his money and Pamela shoots him.
2. Quentin hands over his money and Pamela does not shoot him.
3. Quentin gives Pamela nothing and Pamela shoots him.
4. Quentin gives Pamela nothing and Pamela does not shoot him.
5. Quentin overpowers Pamela and takes away her gun.
6. Pamela overpowers Quentin and takes his money.

Let us assume, for the sake of simplicity, that these six are the only possible outcomes: Quentin has no hidden weapon, there is nothing for him to dive beneath for cover, no police cars are going to appear from around the corner, and so forth. Cases such as this, simpleminded as it is, are perhaps all too familiar by now as examples of coercion. But what is it, precisely, that makes for coercion in such a situation? What must happen in order for coercion to occur? The answer to this question will lead us from the preliminary observations of the preceding chapter to a definition of coercion.

We may observe, first of all, that if Pamela relies on her threat to influence Quentin's action, she has chosen one of the outcomes other than (6). This is not to say that (6) is not a possibility, nor even that she may not have it in mind even while she makes the threat. But if she decides to try to bring about (6), she will have abandoned coercion and turned instead to physical compulsion.

Presumably Pamela wants to avoid outcome (5), which is from her point of view the worst possible outcome. We may infer from her behavior that she wants the money, which is to say that she prefers both (1) and (2) over either (3) or (4). This preference, however, is inessential to the coercive situation. Pamela may be a sufficiently moral person to prefer (4) over (3), or she may be such a monster as to prefer shooting Quentin over letting him live, regardless of whether he gives her his money or not. Such preferences do not affect the character of the threat which Pamela has made, for the threat consists simply in Pamela's having declared the intention of bringing about either (2) or (3), depending on Quentin's response.

What are Quentin's preferences as regards the outcomes we have enumerated? If he has the normal sorts of motivations—he is neither purely altruistic nor suicidally despondent—we may assume that he prefers not to lose his money, but he is even more strongly attached to his life. (1) and (3) are therefore by far the worst outcomes from his standpoint. He would welcome outcome (5), though he may not want to risk trying to achieve it; and he prefers (4) over (2) and prefers (2), by a larger margin, over (1) and (3). But of course Quentin cannot choose between (1) and (2) or between (3) and (4), since the difference between them lies in Pamela's action and not in his. Similarly, Pamela cannot choose between (1) and (3) or between (2) and (4).

What choices can Quentin make in this situation? First, he may try to overpower Pamela, bringing about outcome (5). If he succeeds, the attempt at coercion will have failed. Second, he may refuse to hand over this money, thus bringing about either (3) or (4). This course of action, too, results in the failure of Pamela's attempt to coerce him. Third, he may hand over his money, ensuring outcome (1) or (2). In the last case, provided that he has handed over his money in order to avoid being shot, he will have been coerced. The situation described is one in which a coercive threat has been made—or more precisely, since coercion will occur only if Quentin chooses the third course of action, a potentially coercive threat.

Quentin's preference among the six possible outcomes is for (4), getting away with both his money and his life. But because of the threat Pamela has made he must assume that the result of his decision whether to hand over his money will be either (2) or (3), and in order to avoid (3) he is likely to choose (2). (Let us assume that he does not believe he can successfully overpower Pamela.) The situation is (potentially) coercive because Pamela has threatened Quentin, which is to say that she has declared a conditional intention to harm Quentin only if he does not comply with her demand.

Pamela's intentions alone would not have constituted coercion unless they had been declared, either verbally or by Pamela's actions. On the other hand, Pamela may coerce Quentin even if she has no intention of carrying out her threat, provided that Quentin does not realize that the threat is insincere. If Pamela remarks, while counting out Quentin's money, "That was just a joke—I never intended to shoot you," Quentin has been coerced all the same.

In the situation we have described, the alternative *actions* available to Quentin are just the same as they would have been without the threat. If Pamela had said nothing and shown no intention of harming Quentin, Quentin would still have been able to choose between giving her his money and giving her nothing (or, for that matter, beating her up). But Quentin's *choices*, as he perceives them, are not the same. If Pamela and Quentin had merely encountered one another on the street, it is possible that he would have deliberated whether to give her the contents of his wallet. He would expect either (2) or (4) to result from whichever action he took. Moreover, if Pamela had accosted him and pleaded with him for money, the expected outcome of his actions would have been unchanged. His choices would be the same: to give her money or not to do so. But after Pamela threatens him, Quentin must choose with the expectation that either (2) or (3) will result. Quentin's choices are no longer the same, since the expected outcomes among which he must now choose have been altered by the threat.

The effect on the victim, clearly, is quite different in coercion than in cases of compulsion. Coercion does not take away the victim's *freedom to act*, as does compulsion; but it does diminish or destroy the *freedom to choose*. Threats alter the character of the actions available and their expected consequences, and in this way they leave their victims fewer effective choices than they would otherwise have.

We are now in a position to sum up the features that mark the occurrence of coercion in a revised definition. Several considerations have been identified which make a threat coercive: the threat is credible, the harm threatened extremely serious, and the act demanded is not so undesirable as to rule out the option of complying. We can now formulate a revision of our earlier definition (D1) which includes these elements:

(D2) P coerces Q to do A if and only if
 (i) Q does A, and
 (ii) Q does A because P credibly threatens Q with intolerable harm if he fails to do A.

Threatening in the second clause has its usual meaning, which Nozick has formulated carefully. Briefly, its meaning is this: one person threatens another if he declares his intention to bring about or have brought about a consequence, conditional on the other's acting or failing to act in a certain way, which he believes the other would prefer to avoid.[1]

(D2), I believe, better accounts for the central cases of coercion than does any of the definitions discussed previously. It leaves open the question of whether coercion is justified in a particular case, rather than including illegitimacy as a defining condition as does Dahl. It does not require, as does Frankfurt's and Dworkin's definition, that the motive for a coerced action to an irresistible or unwanted desire. Of the accounts discussed above, Nozick's is the closest to the definition I have proposed, and I am assuming that his account of the nature of threats is correct; but by requiring the threat to be one of intolerable harm (D2) excludes, as Nozick does not, cases of noncoercive duress.[2]

Before exploring in the next chapter the connection of coercion, so understood, with freedom and responsibility, let me comment in light of the preceding discussion on three aspects of the definition: first, its reference to the motivation of the person coerced; second, the meaning of the requirement that the threatened harm be intolerable; and third, the effect of coercion on the will.

First, motivation: the victim of coercion acts *because of* the threatened harm. It is not sufficient for coercion that a penalty have been attached to failure to do an action and that the person thereafter do the action, since he might do so for quite other reasons. It is always possible, as Frankfurt points out, for a person confronted with a threat to ignore the threat and decide how to act without regard for its having been made.[3] Quentin, in our example, might have resolved before setting out on his walk to give all his cash to the first stranger he met—out of benevolence, or for the sake of a tax break on the loss—and might proceed to do so without regard to Pamela's threat. Such a motivation is highly unlikely, to be sure, but not impossible. If he acts with some such motive, then although his action complies with the threat he has not been coerced. The threatener has failed to affect the behavior of her victim (even though she may not realize it), and her attempt at coercion has failed.

We have observed above that there is an unavoidably subjective element in the judgment of whether a threat is sufficient to coerce: a coercive threat is one which is intolerable to the particular individual threatened. Motive introduces a further element of subjectivity into the determination of whether a person is coerced. The motive of wishing to avoid the threatened penalty is seldom absent—it is a remarkable person who can disregard the threat of substantial harm. But when it *is* absent, coercion does not occur.

I turn, second, to the tolerability of the threatened penalty. This must reflect an assessment of the severity of the harm in light of the action demanded. But what is intolerable harm? When is a penalty sufficient to coerce? To answer these questions, I think, we need to consider a few more imaginary examples.

Suppose Adam, a gun in his hand, says to Beth, "Make a face at Charles or I'll kill you," and Beth does so. Clearly she is coerced. The definition is obviously satisfied in this case: being killed is an intolerable cost of refraining from making a face at someone. But if Adam says, "Kill Charles or I'll make a face at you," and Beth complies, she cannot claim coercion as a defense of her act. The harm threatened is trivial, and the act is a grave wrong.

What if Adam says, "Make a face at Charles or I'll make a face at you"? Beth cannot claim to be coerced in this case either; she is subject only to a mild and peculiar sort of duress. But what if the threat is, "Kill him or I'll kick you"? Or "Kick him or I'll kick you"? Still there is no possibility of coercion. Although a harm is threatened, it is a tolerable cost of refraining from killing, or from kicking, another person.

Suppose instead that Adam threatens, "Kill Charles or I'll kill you." Now the penalty threatened is a grave harm, and so is the act demanded. Even so, I do not believe it constitutes a coercive threat. Some acts cannot be coerced, because some acts are so gravely wrong that no threatened penalty, however severe, is an intolerable cost of refusing to comply. The judgments of blame that we make in such cases, I believe, can be seen to support this view.[4] Were Beth to offer Adam's threat as a defense of having killed Charles, we would hold her less blameworthy than if she had killed in cold blood, but we would not excuse her from blame. But coercion cancels blame, even if it does not entirely cancel responsibility for an act. The threat, therefore, is not a coercive threat.[5]

Determination that a threat is coercive requires a weighing of the harm threatened and of the act demanded. If the action demanded harms no one (e.g., the threatener demands that his victim sing the national anthem or press the doorbell) then the threat of any substantial harm is sufficient to coerce. The harm might be physical (a broken finger, a beating) or it might be harm of some other kind ("Do the dishes or I'll tell the papers about you and the mayor's wife"). We have a moral duty not to do harm, but we have no moral duty not to do things we dislike doing. Therefore, *any* serious threat may coerce a person to do a distasteful but harmless act.

If the act demanded involves harming a person, however, coercion can occur only if the threatened penalty is not merely a substantial harm but an intolerable cost of omitting that action. "Drown that child or I'll tell the papers about you and the mayor" is not a coercive threat.

The harm demanded need not be a harm to someone else. One can be coerced to harm oneself, subject to the same balancing of penalty against act. A person who injects himself with heroin out of fear of losing favor with a friend is not coerced, but one who does so under a threat to his life is coerced.

Indeed, a coercive threat need not be a threat of harm to the person coerced: a terrorist may coerce me to hand over my life's savings by threatening to kill his hostages, whether the hostages are members of my family or strangers to me. Indeed, bizarre as it seems, it is possible to coerce another by threatening to harm oneself. "If you see that woman again I'll kill myself" may be a coercive threat, even though the harm it threatens is only secondarily, if at all, a harm to the person who is coerced.

It is difficult to give a precise formulation of the standard of tolerability which distinguishes coercive threats from threats insufficient to coerce. Nevertheless some features of that standard are evident. First, only the threat of substantial harm can coerce; trivial or insignificant threats cannot coerce even a similarly trivial action. Second, a threat to harm a person in a certain way is insufficient to coerce him to harm another in the same way. For to treat others with the respect due to persons requires willingness to risk undergoing harm rather than inflict the same degree of harm on another. The threat of a broken leg cannot coerce me to break another's leg, nor can the threat of death coerce me to kill another—though these cases fall close to the line which distinguishes coercion from noncoercive duress. Rather, a threat which is genuinely coercive must threaten me with a harm substantially greater than any harm I will inflict by complying with the threat.[6]

Coerciveness is determined by the harm which the victim *believes* has been threatened, not by the seriousness of the actual harm threatened. Clearly it is possible to coerce by bluffing or by threatening what the victim mistakenly believes is a serious harm. ("Stand against the wall or I'll shoot you with this gun," said while holding a convincing-looking cap pistol.) Moreover, all of the subjective conditions mentioned earlier must be taken into account in determining whether a threat is coercive, since what is sufficient to coerce one person may not be a coercive threat to a braver person, or to a person without the victim's particular fears and sensitivities. The threat must pose an intolerable cost *to the victim*. An intolerable cost is one which we cannot reasonably expect the particular individual threatened—not an ideally rational agent in his place—to accept as a cost of defying the threat.

Third, and finally, definition (D2) identifies the way in which coercion interferes with the victim's will. The victim of coercion wills to act as he does, and yet he is not free to choose a course of action in the normal way.[7] The threat determines his will to choose the action demanded, overcoming all other reasons—moral principles, goals, desires, and inclinations—which would otherwise influence him. It is not necessary to coercion, as some have claimed, that the victim be forced to act *against* his will.[8] Nevertheless coercion interferes with the victim's will—whatever the relation of the coerced act to his antecedent intentions—by making his intentions and wishes irrelevant to the determination of his action.[9]

Offers and Threats

Definition (D2) above makes reference only to the *threat* of intolerable consequences. Is it possible, as some writers have suggested, that *offers* as well as threats may be coercive?[10]

It seems that they may. If Priscilla finds Quirinius about to drown and offers to save him on condition that he do some action A, Quirinius may claim that he is coerced to do A. If he is on the point of starvation and Priscilla offers him food only if he will do something he prefers not to do, again he may claim to be coerced.

What distinguishes such situations from other offers is that to forego the benefit offered is to suffer an intolerable harm. The "offer" made by Priscilla in either case described is unlike other offers in that failure to carry it out would gravely harm the person to whom the offer is made. Characteristic of such situations are two features: first, the benefit offered is one of which the potential recipient is in immediate need; and, second, it is a benefit for which he is dependent on the maker of the offer.[11]

Under such circumstances offers may be coercive. But they might just as aptly be described as situations in which Priscilla threatens Quirinius—threatens to let him drown or starve. We would not describe an ordinary offer as a threat, however. If Paula offers Quincy a thousand dollars to appear in her movie, we could not reasonably say she has threatened to withhold a thousand dollars from him unless he takes the part.

With some imagination we can make even such an ordinary offer coercive. What if Quincy needs the thousand dollars to pay for an hour on the kidney dialysis machine and has no other way of getting it?[12] Then we would grant Quincy's claim to have been coerced, if the matter comes into question—if the movie is pornographic and Quincy has to explain his appearance in it to a court or to his mother, for example. Even so, it seems to strain the ordinary sense of the term "threat" to say that Paula has threatened Quincy by making her offer, coercive as, under the circumstances, it proves to be.

It seems reasonable to conclude, therefore, that offers can sometimes be coercive. The definition offered above requires that coercion arise from a threat, however, and it applies to such cases only if we extend the concept of a threat in an implausible way. We may accommodate such cases, however, by revising (D2) thus:

(D3) P coerces Q to do A if and only if
    (i) Q does A, and
    (ii) Q does A because P credibly tells Q that, in order to get Q to do A, P will bring it about that Q can avoid intolerable harm only by doing A.[13]

On this revised definition the offers we have been discussing, offers made in circumstances which leave a person no reasonable alternative but to accept in order to avoid intolerable harm, can be seen as bringing about coercion in precisely the same way as do threats. Normally, of course, the difference between offers and threats is obvious and morally significant: a person who makes an offer leaves the other person the option of refusing the offer and remaining as she is, whereas the maker of a threat forces the other person to choose between two unwanted outcomes. But when the offer is of something essential for one's well-being, and when no other offers are available, an offer functions exactly as does a coercive threat by leaving no reasonable alternative.

A Semantic Map

Before leaving the concept of coercion and turning to its moral evaluation, we should say something about the location of this concept in respect to certain related concepts. How does coercion differ from other means of influencing or controlling others' behavior?

First, let us consider the closely related terms "force" and "violence." *Force*, as a substantive, refers to physical constraint or compulsion. A kidnapper who wrestles his victim into a car and ties him up to prevent him from leaving is employing force, as is a police officer who physically restrains someone from entering a building. An army employs force of several kinds in occupying a territory or defending its position.

The verb *to force* has a much wider use, and it is possible to force a person to do something without employing force. To force a person to act is to compel her to act in a particular way. Coercion is one of the ways in which this can be accomplished: coercion causes a person to act in a particular way by threatening intolerable consequences if she does not. But coercion need not involve the application of force.

Some definitions of coercion make force essential to coercion. The *Oxford English Dictionary* offers as a definition "the application of force to control the action of a voluntary agent."[14] J. R. Lucas suggests that "a man is being coerced when either force is being used against him or his behavior is being determined by the threat of force."[15] Such definitions are too restrictive. It is possible to coerce a person by threatening to make damaging disclosures about him, for example, without either using or threatening force. The error arises, no doubt, from the fact that many of the cases of coercion which are of concern to us do involve the threat of force.

Both *force* and *coercion* are sometimes used in a sense which includes a final moral evaluation, so that "justified force" and "justified coercion" are regarded as self-contradictory. A claim that a person has employed force or coercion is sometimes countered by a claim that what he did was justified, thus implicitly invoking a moral definition.

I do not intend to use the terms in such a sense, however, and I do not believe that common usage requires that we do so. When we have determined whether an action is an instance of force or coercion, we have not yet settled the question of whether it is a justified action. All the same, as I shall argue below, there is a moral presumption against coercion, a presumption which must be overcome in cases of justified coercion.

Coercion, unlike *force*, is a term whose application is in a certain sense dependent on normative criteria. For in order to judge whether a person has been coerced to do an act it is necessary to determine whether the penalty threatened was sufficient in light of the act demanded to make it unreasonable to defy the threat. And this requires judgments both of the severity of the penalty and of how objectionable the act demanded is. In labelling a threat coercive, in other words, we are implicitly making the judgment not merely that severe harm is at stake but that a person cannot be expected to disregard such a threat—a judgment which has obvious normative force.

Dependence on a prior normative judgment is not, I think, a weakness of a definition of coercion. Such dependence is to be expected: coercion is, after all, a moral concept, one of the categories we use in sorting out and evaluating human actions, and it should be no surprise that its application in a particular case is always dependent on another moral judgment. But the question of whether a threat is justified remains open even when it is clearly a coercive threat, for the issue of justification is not the same as the issue of whether the person threatened is in fact coerced. It would be misleading, therefore, to define coercion in a way which entails moral condemnation.

Violence, in contrast, has an ineliminable evaluative aspect.[16] Violence is force or coercion wrongfully employed. In the terms which John Ladd uses to summarize Kant's understanding of violence, it is "the illegitimate use of coercion."[17] To say that one person has employed violent means in order to affect the actions of another is to say that he has employed force or coercion in an illegitimate way, forcing the other to act by morally objectionable means. Violence also refers more broadly to acts of deliberate destruction or injury, whether or not they are intended as means of affecting others' actions. A group which shifts its tactics from persuasion and political agitation to bombings is employing violence, even if the bombings are not undertaken as ways to cause others to do certain acts.

Violence, then, is a morally condemnatory term which can be applied to various forms of coercion or direct harm. It is not a distinct category of interpersonal action but rather a label connoting disapproval of actions which may fall under any of several categories.

We have already noted that *compulsion* differs from coercion in that it involves the use of force upon the person. The victim of compulsion does not act at all; he, or his body, is the instrument by which the other acts. There is also another way of interfering with another's acts, similar to compulsion except that it hinders rather than compels action, and that is *disablement*. Disablement takes away not the opportunity but the necessary means to do a certain act or range of acts. A person may be prevented from stealing by the once-common practice of cutting off his hands or by the more current technique of aversion therapy. What is loosely called "brainwashing"—if in fact it is ever successful—does not coerce but disables its victim, since its purpose is to make the victim unable to remember or consider reasons for acting in nonconforming ways.

Persuasion is another means of influencing behavior. It resembles coercion rather than compulsion in that its purpose is to bring about certain intentional acts, but it differs from coercion in leaving the agent free to choose his actions. Persuasion attempts to provide a person with new reasons for actions or to call attention to existing reasons, but it does not do this in such a way as to exclude all choices but one. To persuade another is not to alter the choices available to the agent but to point out antecedent features which, the persuader hopes, will affect his choice of action. Since persuasion aims to influence but not to transform the normal process by which we decide how to act, it does not interfere with the will as does coercion. An act which one is persuaded to perform, unlike a coerced act, is a fully voluntary act.

Persuasion and reasoning may take place, however, against a background which includes coercive elements. When persuasion gains force from such a background, it does diminish the freedom of the agent to choose his action. Gert has provided a helpful catalogue of various kinds of "impure" reasoning.[18] If P urges Q to pay his taxes in order to avoid going to jail, then P's attempt to persuade Q has a coercive background even though P is not coercing Q; P's argument draws force from the existence of a coercive institution.[19] If, in addition, it is within P's power to prevent the harm of which he warns Q— if, for example, P is a tax inspector with the power to open or close Q's case—then P's reasoning with Q contains elements of coercion. P is then attempting to coerce Q, though he may also be reasoning with him. Each of these is a case in which Q's freedom to choose a course of action is narrowed by the coercive aspects of the reasons which P offers.

There are at least two other modes of influencing behavior which fall between coercion and persuasion. *Duress* has already been discussed: it consists in the threat of consequences which, though undesirable, are not intolerable and hence are insufficient to coerce. *Enticement* is the offer of benefits. Duress and enticement are alike in that they seek to influence behavior by attaching consequences to alternative actions available to the agent. They thus alter the character of the acts from among which the agent must choose. But the alternative actions which were open to the agent before the threat or offer remain reasonable alternatives, and so duress and enticement fall short of compelling the action which the person employing them desires. Under conditions of duress and enticement a person's responsibility for his actions is mitigated but by no means eliminated.

We may sum up this discussion of various means of influencing behavior by arranging them in an order which reflects at the same time increasing likelihood of effectiveness, increasing interference with the normal operation of the subject's will, and diminishing responsibility of the subject for a resulting action:

Suggestion
Persuasion
Enticement

Duress
Persuasion against a coercive background
Persuasion with coercive elements
Coercion
Compulsion and disablement

Because of the increasing severity of interference with an individual's will, each of these modes of influence must overcome a stronger presumption against its employment than the ones earlier on the list. In order to understand the nature and the ground of the moral case against coercion, however, it is necessary to examine more closely the relationship between the concept of coercion and the conditions for moral responsibility. It is to that task that we turn in the next chapter.

Notes

1. Nozick, "Coercion," 444–45, 447–58. I do not here take account of Nozick's elaborate distinctions among threats, offers, and warnings, but I return to some of these matters immediately below.
2. Clause (i) of (D1) is identical to Nozick's condition (4), except that I have stated conditions for being coerced to do something rather than being coerced to refrain from an action. Nozick's conditions (1), (2), (5), and (6) are condensed into clause (ii), with the further qualification that the threat be one of intolerable harm. I have omitted Nozick's (3) and (3'), the eventually very complicated condition describing P's intentions; in standard cases P's intentions are clear enough from his having made a threat.
3. Frankfurt, "Coercion and Moral Responsibility," p 82.
4. Issues of blameworthiness and responsibility are discussed, and the position which I take here is defended, in chap. 4, below.
5. Suppose that Beth had killed Adam instead—assuming that his threat was credible and that there appeared to be no other way of preventing him from carrying out his threat. Beth could then claim to have killed in self-defense, which is a legal defense and, on many conceptions of morality, a moral excuse. But the same defense cannot be offered for killing Charles; no one can kill an innocent party in self-defense.
6. The harm must be "substantially greater" in order to rule out a threat such as, "Go steal $1000 from that man or I'll take $1100 from you." If equal losses represent equal harms, such a threat is not coercive.
7. Frankfurt, "Coercion and Moral Responsibility," p 80: "The victim of coercion is either moved in some way against his will or his will is in some way circumvented. . . ."
8. Christian Bay defines coercion as "the application of sanctions sufficiently strong to make the individual abandon a course of action or inaction dictated by his own strong and enduring motives or wishes." But this condition need not be met: one can be coerced to perform an action to which one has only a mild and temporary aversion or to which one is indifferent. One may even be coerced to do something one would have done, for different reasons, without the threat. See Christian Bay, *The Structure of Freedom* (Stanford: Stanford University Press, 1958), p 93. This is Bay's second sense of coercion, since he includes physical compulsion—"the application of actual physical violence"—as the first clause of his definition of coercion.
9. It is in this sense, also, that Frankfurt's claim that "coercion must always involve a violation of the victim's autonomy," quoted earlier, should be understood. Autonomy as Frankfurt here uses the term is the ability to shape one's future by one's own choices, and this ability is taken away by coercive threats. The effect on autonomy is a consequence of the defining conditions of coercion stated above.

10. See Frankfurt, "Coercion and Moral Responsibility," 66–75; Virginia Held, "Coercion and Coercive Offers," in J. Roland Pennock and John W. Chapman, eds., *Coercion, Nomos*, vol. 14 (Chicago: Aldine Atherton Co., 1972), 49–62.

11. Frankfurt cites these two conditions as necessary to make an offer into a threat and adds a third: that the maker of the offer exploit the potential recipient's need and dependency by demanding an unfair or improper price for the benefit he offers. But this is not necessary. A drowning man might be coerced to pay a dollar to his rescuer for the fuel expended in bringing him to shore. That the recipient pays a fair price, even a bargain price, for the benefit he needs does not affect the coerciveness of the situation. See Frankfurt, "Coercion and Moral Responsibility," 71–72.

12. I owe this and several other outlandish counterexamples to the feverish imagination of Charles R. Beitz.

13. This formulation, in place of a disjunctive definition to cover threats and offers in separate clauses, was suggested by T. M. Scanlon. Note that I am not here attempting to define when an offer amounts to a threat; my interest is in the much narrower class of offers which constitute *coercive* threats.

14. *Oxford English Dictionary*, compact ed. (New York: Oxford University Press, 1971), s.v. "coercion."

15. John Randolph Lucas, *The Principles of Politics* (New York: Oxford University Press, 1966), p. 60.

16. I have in mind " violence" in its specific application to the actions of people on other people, not in the broader sense of intensity or rapidity (e.g., "violent motion").

17. John Ladd, "Translator's Introduction" to Immanuel Kant, *The Metaphysical Elements of Justice* (Indianapolis: Bobbs-Merrill, 1965), p xix.

18. Gert, "Coercion and Freedom," 44–47.

19. This is not precisely Gert's criterion. According to Gert, P's reasoning with Q has a coercive background when P believes that someone else in stating the same facts would be coercing Q. Gert's condition is also satisfied in the example given above.

4
COERCION AND RESPONSIBILITY

We turn now from the nature of coercion to its moral status and its bearing on the moral assessment of acts. In this brief chapter I shall discuss the consequences of coercion for moral responsibility, in the following chapter its connection with freedom. In a longer fifth chapter I will construct an account of both the presumption against coercion and the circumstances which justify it on the basis of a general account of rights.

To be responsible for an action is to be accountable or answerable for the action and its consequences. An act for which one is responsible is an act which is one's own—an act which is morally good, bad, or indifferent. Moral responsibility includes liability to be praised or blamed for the action, if the action itself is praiseworthy or blameworthy.

Responsibility involves more than simple causation. If a collision has occurred at sea, in trying to explain it we might say either.

    1. "The captain of the *Pequod* was responsible for the collision."
or
    2. "Malfunctioning navigational equipment was responsible for the collision."

(Responsibility might be shared, of course, but let us take these as asserting full responsibility and hence as mutually exclusive.) (2) simply asserts a causal relation; it says just the same thing as

    3. "Malfunctioning navigational equipment caused the collision."

In contrast, (1) does not say exactly what is said by

    4. "The captain of the *Pequod* caused the collision."

For (4) might be true even if (1) is false. Suppose, for example, that the collision occurred after the captain had made a change of course and thereby sailed into the path of a submarine, which was just surfacing but had not disclosed its location by radio to other vessels. The captain would then have caused the collision by making the change of course: without his action the collision would not have occurred. Yet— taking responsibility in the broadly moral sense it has in common usage—it would be misleading to say that the captain was responsible for the collision. The outcome depended causally upon his actions, but responsibility lies elsewhere.

(4) may even be false in circumstances where (1) is true, if we include other senses of responsibility besides moral responsibility. The captain may be legally responsible for the collision even if he was off the bridge and sleeping when it occurred. The corporation which owns the ship may bear civil liability, one of several categories of legal responsibility, for the collision and its consequences even though its causal connections with the actual events are extremely remote.

Moral responsibility includes causation, but it requires more besides. The captain is morally responsible only if he not only caused the collision by his action but also had sufficient information to know that this was what he was doing. Furthermore, both of these conditions may be present and yet responsibility for the act absent if his act was not voluntary—if the captain was insane at the time, for example, or was subjected to compulsion. Aristotle stated the conditions for voluntary action thus: "Since that which is done under compulsion or by reason of ignorance is involuntary, the voluntary would seem to be that of which the moving principle is in the agent himself, he being aware of the particular circumstances of the action."[1]

Responsibility of an agent for an act requires that the act be a voluntary act. Voluntary acts are acts which are done consciously, intentionally, and as a result of the agent's decision. More precisely, the following two conditions are necessary and jointly sufficient for moral responsibility:

(i) The agent knows what he is doing, i.e., knows what his act is and what are its likely consequences; and

(ii) The act results from the agent's choice among the alternative actions open to him.

Exactly what is required for an act to "result from an agent's choice" can be accounted for, I shall assume, by either a deterministic or a nondeterministic theory of choice and action. A nondeterminist will identify voluntary actions as actions which are not causally necessitated by preexisting conditions; a determinist will hold that voluntary actions, though like all others they are causally determined, differ in that the causal process which brings them about is one which is particularly important to us or one with which we identify ourselves.

Acts performed negligently may appear to provide counterexamples to this account of responsibility. For persons are held responsible for negligent actions even if they did not know what they were doing when they acted, thus failing to satisfy the condition (i).

But what one is responsible *for* in cases of negligence is acting without regard for probable consequences. The negligent person is not directly responsible for the harm which results from his act, but he is responsible for going about some activity or other without awareness of its possibly harmful consequences. It is precisely his *lack* of awareness that is blameworthy. And that may be just as serious a wrong, morally and legally, as the direct and intentional infliction of harm.

Responsibility for Coerced Acts

Acts performed under coercion satisfy both of the conditions for responsibility stated above. A person coerced to do an act knows what he is doing, and his act results from his choice, from among the alternatives open to him, to comply with the coercer's demands rather than risk the threatened penalty. A coerced act, therefore, is an act for which the agent is responsible.

But it is misleading to speak of responsibility *tout court* rather than of responsibility *under the circumstances*. And the circumstances of coerced acts are radically different from the circumstances of most other acts.

Under coercive circumstances, because the threatened penalty is an intolerable cost of defying the threat, submission is the only reasonable course of action. The robbery victim whose life is threatened has no reasonable choice but to hand over her money. What she is responsible for is giving up her money under those circumstances.

Furthermore, by leaving only one reasonable choice open to the agent, coercion *absolves the victim from praise or blame* for her act. That a person did a morally bad act under coercion is no indication of bad character, since the coercer left her no reasonable choice but to do so. That a coerced act is virtuous does not reflect the virtue of the agent, since she was moved to act by fear of undergoing an intolerable penalty. For the same reason it is inappropriate either to punish or to reward a person for something which she was coerced to do.

If anyone deserves blame for coerced actions it is the coercer, not the victim. The coercer bears a greater share of the responsibility than does his victim for the victim's actions, since the actions depend to a greater degree on his choice than on that of the victim.

The picture we have sketched thus far may appear incorrect in light of the possibility that a person may be criticized, and properly so, for submitting to coercion. A man who betrays a friend's trust because of a blackmail threat, or a woman who assists in a fraudulent investment scheme under a threat of being beaten, may be blamed for what they do. Do not such examples disprove the claim that coerced acts do not deserve blame?

Criticism of such a person might be intended in either of two ways. First, a person who *claims* to have been coerced may be criticized because the threatened penalty was *not* intolerable in light of the action demanded. An observer may conclude, notwithstanding the victim's testimony to the contrary, that the threat constituted not coercion but only duress. If this is the force of the criticism, the victim is not actually being blamed for an action done under coercion but is being faulted for yielding inappropriately to noncoercive influences.

Second, even a person who genuinely is coerced may be blamed because he ought to have had the strength of character necessary to defy the threat. The agent may be blamed because a courageous person, or even a person of normal moral fortitude, would in the same circumstances have refused to comply. But in this case the victim is blamed not for acting as he did, given his character, but for failing to develop a less vulnerable character. There is nothing improper about criticizing a person for certain traits of his character, to the extent that it is within his power to alter them.[2] It would be improper, however, to ascribe blame for the coerced act itself.

How does the effect of coercion on responsibility compare with the effect of other circumstances in which the normal means of influencing our actions are blocked? A person who acts while insane, for example, does not know what she is doing and does not intentionally choose her act; she is not responsible for her action. Someone who is either physically compelled to act or acts as a result of psychological compulsion, though she knows what she is doing, does not act on the basis of a free choice; and so such acts also fail to meet the conditions for responsibility. Such a person might be responsible for failing to free herself from her psychological conditions, if it is within her power to do so; or she might be responsible for placing herself in a situation where she is likely to be compelled to do something wrong. For her particular act, however, she is not responsible.

What about a person who is compelled by physical circumstances to act in a certain way? An example (similar to one mentioned by Frankfurt and cited in a previous chapter) is the man who takes a detour because he knows that his continuing to walk on the path he is now following will trigger an avalanche. Such a person is like the victim of coercion in that he acts with responsibility for his actions in a situation where the course of action he previously intended to take is no longer a reasonable choice. As in the case of coercion, it is inappropriate to praise or blame him for the act which he saw to be the only reasonable one; but the responsibility for his act is not shared, as in the case of coercion, with someone else.

The two conditions set out above, then, serve to identify the circumstances in which we are responsible for our actions. Since they are satisfied in the case of coercion, coerced acts fall within the category of morally responsible actions, even though praise and blame are inappropriate.

Moral and Legal Responsibility

It is frequently said that coerced acts are acts for which the agent is not responsible. Frankfurt, for example, equates "being genuinely coerced" with "bearing no responsibility for one's submission to a threat."[3]

I believe this is a mistake. Because a coerced act is the result of deliberate choice with awareness of probable consequences, it is an act for which one is morally responsible. Coercion diminishes but does not annul moral responsibility. The victim of coercion is responsible for his act, but what he is responsible for is doing such act *under coercion*.

Coercion *does* render praise and blame for an action inappropriate, however. When we judge that a person has done some action under coercion, we at the same time ascribe moral responsibility for the act to him—we recognize it as his act—and deny the applicability of praise and blame. A person who keeps a promise only because he is threatened with violence if he does not deserves no commendation for keeping his promise, nor is it appropriate to blame a person who breaks a promise if she is coerced to do so. Coerced acts are not acts for which we deserve moral credit, because coercion changes the character of an act. A normally blameworthy act done under coercion is not blameworthy.

If, as some theories of ethics would have it, moral responsibility simply *is* liability to be praised or blamed for an act, then the above account is incoherent.[4] But this objection can be turned back on itself: circumstances of coercion provide a counterexample to the claim that responsibility is blameworthiness, for coerced acts are responsible but not blameworthy acts. Therefore—and this way of speaking seems a reasonable extension of common usage—not all responsible acts are liable to praise or blame.

Although moral responsibility is not annulled by coercion, if the account I have offered is correct, the effect of coercion on legal responsibility is different. Coercion usually *does* negate legal responsibility, and evidence that a person acted under coercion releases him from legal responsibility for the act. A person who disobeys traffic laws at gunpoint will not be punished for doing so. At issue in Patty Hearst's trial for participating in bank robberies, to cite a familiar example, was precisely the question of whether she was coerced to do so and hence not legally responsible.

This difference in application makes clearer the essential difference between these two concepts of responsibility. Moral responsibility admits as relevant whatever evidence may exist concerning the doing of the act, for what is in question is simply whether a particular act is the person's own act. Legal responsibility requires further that it be the person's act under specified circumstances which render him liable to legal action. Moral responsibility has to do not just with praise and blame but deals also at a more fundamental level with how we credit acts to persons. It is a conceptual tool that we use in categorizing events into natural occurrences and acts of persons. It can be said, therefore, that a person is morally responsible for what would normally be an evil act, in the sense that the act is his act, and yet not to be blamed for it. And this is precisely the moral status of coerced acts.

We need to qualify what has been said concerning legal responsibility, however, by noting the difference between two kinds of legal responsibility. Above I have taken legal responsibility to mean liability to be punished for an act, or in other words criminal liability to prosecution and punishment. Responsibility of this kind is absent in cases of coercion. But legal responsibility also includes civil liability, liability to be subject to civil action by others for recovery of damages. Under present statutes, there are some cases of civil liability, and even a few cases of criminal liability, in which lack of intention does not cancel legal responsibility. When laws mandate the standard of "strict liability" for a particular offense, for example, neither ignorance or inadvertence is a legal excuse. A person who sells tainted milk or adulterated drugs is not excused, according to existing laws, by his ignorance that he was doing so, even when his ignorance did not arise from negligence or failure to take adequate precautions. I am not aware that strict liability statutes have ever been applied to cases of coercion. But since neither willful wrongdoing nor negligence is required for conviction under such statutes, it appears that a coerced act might be legally a responsible act, for purposes both of criminal prosecution and of civil suit, under such laws.[5]

In normal cases, however, coercion cancels legal but not moral responsibility. I have argued above that coercion renders an act exempt from moral praise or blame. And this is the reason for the annulment of legal responsibility: legal responsibility, or at any rate criminal responsibility, is coextensive with—perhaps essentially identical to—

liability to sanctions of one kind or another. To judge a person legally responsible for a crime is to judge that he deserves punishment, which is the institutionalized legal counterpart of moral blame.[6]

For this reason among others, moral responsibility is far more inclusive than legal responsibility. In the first place, all actions about which the law is silent are actions to which moral responsibility may apply but on which legal responsibility has no bearing. There are also special situations in which legal responsibility is cancelled. An undercover informant may be granted immunity from prosecution for illegal acts he commits in order to make his cover convincing. No one has the authority, however, to absolve him from moral accountability for those acts.

Furthermore—to turn to the case which particularly concerns us—coerced acts are acts to which moral responsibility applies but criminal liability does not. The effect of coercion can be clarified by comparing it with another legal excuse. If I claim that I struck someone in self-defense, for example, I am *claiming* moral responsibility for my act. I am asserting that the act was my act, not an inadvertent movement, and that I struck the person deliberately and intentionally. But at the same time I am *disclaiming* criminal responsibility, since my acting in self-defense, if that is indeed what I was doing, excuses me from liability to punishment for the act.

Coercion is similar in this regard to the excuse of self-defense. To say that I did something under coercion is to say that it was my act, an act which I chose from among the alternatives open to me at the time. But it is at the same time to assert that the alternatives had been constricted by another in such a way that I do not deserve either moral blame (or praise) or legal punishment (or reward) for the act. Coerced acts, therefore, are morally but not legally responsible acts.

Our examination of the concept of responsibility and its application to coercion has been brief, since our major interest lies in the moral assessment of coercion itself as a mode of human action. In order to lay the groundwork for a moral theory of coercion, we turn in the next chapter to a discussion of the extent to which coercion deprives its victim of freedom. The question of freedom will lead, in the chapter following, to a general theory of the nature of rights, in light of which the precise nature of the harm which coercion does to us will become clearer.

Notes

1. Aristotle, *Nicomachean Ethics*, III. 1., 1111a. 21–24; trans. W. D. Ross, in J. L. Ackrill, ed., *Aristotle's Ethics* (New York: Humanities Press, 1973), 78.
2. Cf. Aristotle, *Nicomachean Ethics*, II. 2, III. 5; Donald Davidson, "How Is Weakness of

Will Possible?", in Joel Feinberg, ed., *Moral Concepts* (London: Oxford University Press, 1969), 93–113.

   3. Frankfurt, "Coercion and Moral Responsibility," in Ted Honderich, ed., *Essays on Freedom of Action* (Boston: Routledge and Kegan Paul, 1973), 78. The passage was quoted in chapter 2, above.

   4. Frankena states but does not develop such a theory in his brief book, *Ethics*, 2d ed. (Englewood Cliffs, N.J.: Prentice-Hall, 1973), 72. R. B. Brandt proposes a definition of duty in terms of praiseworthiness, which he credits to Wilfred Sellars, in *Ethical Theory* (Englewood Cliffs, N.J.: Prentice Hall, 1959), 358. Such a view of moral responsibility is often rooted in an emotivist theory of ethics; an example of this conjunction is found in A. J. Ayer, *Language, Truth, and Logic* (New York: Dover, 1952), chap. 6.

   5. Another instance in which legal responsibility raises unusual complications, more familiar in law than the relatively uncommon strict liability offenses, has to do with vicarious responsibility for the actions of an authorized agent. When one ship collides with and damages another, the owner of the damaged ship is likely to bring suit not against the ship's captain or crew but against the owner of the ship which caused the damage. The owner of a ship is responsible for damage caused by his ship, as is the employer of a workman for damage done by the workman, even if the owner or employer had no knowledge of what his agent was doing and therefore lacked the conditions necessary for moral responsibility.

   The cases of vicarious responsibility for the acts of agents that I have mentioned are instances of civil liability for recovery of damages. Can criminal liability also be vicariously held? It would seem so. If an accountant prepares a fraudulent tax return for a client, for example, not only the accountant but also the client is liable to prosecution. Or, to take another kind of case, a person who hires another to perform murder is no less guilty of a criminal offense than is the person who performs murder for hire.

   These are not really cases of vicarious criminal responsibility, however. In each case the person who authorizes another's actions is being held legally responsible not for the other's actions but for his own. The person who hires a murderer is guilty of hiring a murderer, not of committing murder. His act is a criminal offense, possibly one even more serious than murder; but it is the agent's act, not another's on his behalf, for which he is liable to prosecution. Similarly, the person who allows a fraudulent tax return to be submitted in his name is guilty of failure to take sufficient care that his return be accurate. His guilt arises not simply from the acts of his agent but from his having signed a fraudulent return. (If he could show that his signature was forged, for example, and that he actually signed an accurate return, he would thereby show his innocence.)

   Genuinely vicarious responsibility, therefore, appears to occur only in civil and not in criminal contexts. Vicarious moral responsibility, properly speaking, is impossible: an act which another performs cannot be *my* act in the sense necessary for moral responsibility. We may seem at times to attribute moral responsibility vicariously: we may blame a parent for the acts of a child or blame the citizens of a nation for the acts of its leaders. But in these cases what we judge blameworthy are not the acts of someone other than the person who bears the blame, but rather actions or omissions of the agent that contribute to or cause other's acts. The parent is blamed for giving poor guidance or failing to exercise proper control over the child; the citizens are blamed for failing to do what they might have done to prevent their leaders from acting as they did or for actively supporting their leaders' acts.

   6. I do not wish to identify punishment with moral blame; my point here is simply that its function in a legal system is very much like the function of blame in moral judgment. The relationship of punishment to morality is discussed at greater length in chapter 10, below.

5
COERCION AND FREEDOM

Coercion is usually counted among the most important obstacles to freedom. Liberty has even been defined as the absence of coercion.[1] But the foregoing examination of the concept of coercion calls this view into question. The person who acts under coercion acts as a result of his choice to submit rather than risk intolerable harm, and surely the making of a choice presupposes freedom. A person who is physically compelled is evidently deprived of his freedom, and yet coercion leaves the victim a decision whether or not to submit.

In order to shed light on the relation between coercion and freedom we shall examine several accounts, both historical and contemporary, of what it is for an agent to be free. My intent is not to construct a complete account of freedom and its significance but rather to draw a clear enough picture of the nature of freedom so that we can identify the way in which coercion destroys or diminishes it.

Locke: Ability to Do What One Will

What is freedom? What does it mean to say that a person is free? According to one account, to be free is to be able to act as one wants to. A person is free if his actions conform to his will and desires. A principal defender of this view is John Locke, in the *Essay Concerning Human Understanding*. Locke asserts that

> the idea of liberty is, the idea of a power in any agent to do or forbear any particular action, according to the determination or thought of the mind. . . .[2]

Locke later expands on this definition:

> I am at liberty to speak or hold my peace; and as far as this power reaches, of acting or not acting, by the determination of his own

thought preferring either, so far is a man free. For how can we think anyone freer, than to have the power to do what he will?[3]

In the latter passage Locke suggests an unusually strict definition of freedom when he defines it as the "power . . . of acting or not acting" as one will. Usually Locke takes it as sufficient for liberty that a person act as he will, whether or not he has the power to refrain.

According to Locke, a person who is constrained to do what he would want to do in any case is free.

> Suppose a man be carried, whilst fast asleep, into a room where is a person he longs to see and speak with; and be there locked in, beyond his power to get out: he awakes, and is glad to find himself in so desirable company, which he stays willingly in, i.e., prefers his stay to going away. I ask, is not his stay voluntary? I think nobody will deny it; and yet, being locked fast in, it is evident that he is not at liberty not to stay, he has not freedom to be gone.[4]

Whether such a person is able to do what he wants to do depends on how we interpret "what he wants to do." As the case is described, what he wants to do is to stay in the room. He is able to do that, and there is no reason to deny that he is free to do so. If freedom in acting requires only that a person be able to do what he wants at the moment to do, the man in the locked room stays there freely.

But this has the unwelcome consequence that a person's freedom may be increased or diminished simply by an alteration in his wants. When a person is compelled to do something he does not want to do, then, according to Locke, his freedom is abridged. But if he subsequently changes his mind and decides that the action he is compelled to perform is desirable after all, he has become free. The point has been forcefully put by Haskell Fain: "There would seem to be two ways of freeing the prisoner. One would be to remove his chains, the other would be to present the prisoner with a copy of Epictetus."[5]

Changing the story will make the inadequacy of this definition still clearer. Suppose that a person is seized while awake, and despite her protests she is locked into a room alone. Some time later another person—someone whom the prisoner admires greatly—is also brought into the room. The first person may now have less reason to complain of her treatment than before. Perhaps the other person imposed these peculiar conditions as the only circumstances under which he would speak with the captive; if so, she may even be grateful to her captors. But none of this makes her *free* while she is staying in the room. She is no more free than she was while she was alone in the room. A change in circumstances has brought her action into conformity with her will, making her able to do what at the moment she wants to do. But this change has not rendered either her or her action free. Were Locke's a correct account of freedom, the freedom of the inmates of the world's prisons would depend on the congeniality of their fellow prisoners.

There are important differences between *acting freely, being free to act*, and *being free*. It might be argued that the man in Locke's example is *staying in the room freely*, since that is, after all, what he now wants to do, and he is doing so. He is *free to stay*, clearly: he is able to stay, and nothing prevents him from staying. But of course he is not *free to leave*, since the doors are locked.

Is the prisoner *free, tout court?* It seems clear that he is not: *being free* requires more than just coincidence of act with present will but requires also that a range of acts be open to the agent without hindrance. The prisoner can stay in the room but cannot leave, and so he is not *free to act*.

A more plausible definition of freedom can be drawn from Locke's account if we take a broader interpretation of the agent's desires: we may take "what the agent wants to do" to refer generally and nonspecifically to any of the range of alternative actions available to the agent. On this revised account, an agent acts freely just in case he is able to do whatever he wants or might want to do. This is evidently not Locke's intended sense of freedom, since it is not satisfied in his example. But this interpretation is suggested by Locke's statement, quoted above, that freedom requires "the power of acting or not acting."

Defining freedom in terms of a person's wants or desires may be misleading, since an individual's desires may be inconsistent or in conflict.[6] We can avoid such ambiguities by speaking instead of the ability to act as one *wills* or *decides* to act. We may formulate the revised quasi-Lockean definition of freedom thus: An agent is free to the extent that he is able to do whatever accords with his will. "Whatever accords with his will" is understood to denote what he now wills or might will to do. The man in the locked room is not free.

According to this account of freedom, everything which prevents a person from acting as he wills diminishes his freedom. But this is surely too sweeping. It has the consequence that human beings, or at any rate those who have a will to fly, are unfree to fly, and that persons who want to become good runners but lack the self-discipline necessary to achieve that condition are unfree to do so.

Lack of freedom should not be confused with inability. Everyone is free to play the *Hammerklavier* sonata on the piano, or for that matter on the accordion. But relatively few persons are able to do the former, and thankfully still fewer to do the latter. A person who studies the piano until he can play the Beethoven sonatas gains an ability he lacked but does not increase his freedom.

The Lockean account of freedom appears unable to support this distinction. Locke's definition treats any obstacle to doing what one will as an obstacle to freedom; but this includes inabilities of every kind as well as genuine limits on liberty. In order to make these distinctions, therefore, we need an account of freedom which makes reference to the way in which will is linked to action.

Hobbes: Absence of External Restraint

Perhaps what distinguishes limits to freedom from other obstacles to action is their *origin*. In the examples mentioned above, inabilities which are part of the person's own physical or psychological nature or condition do not restrict freedom. But if similar restrictions were imposed from without, they would be infringements of freedom. A second major stream of political thought has taken precisely the absence of external interference to be the defining condition of freedom.

Hobbes gives a classic statement of this view in *Leviathan:*

> By Liberty is understood, according to the proper signification of the word, the absence of external Impediments: which Impediments, may oft take away a man's power to do what hee would; but cannot hinder him from using the power left him, according as his judgment, and reason shall dictate to him.[7]

Later Hobbes states:

> A Free-Man is he, that in those things, which by his strength and wit he is able to do, is not hindred to doe what he has a will to do.[8]

Hobbes stresses that this notion of liberty is not applicable only to rational or even animate beings. Indeed, he argues that it applies properly only to bodies:

> Liberty, or Freedome, signifieth (properly) the absence of Opposition; (by Opposition, I mean externall Impediments of motion;) and may be applied no lesse to Irrationall, and Inanimate creatures, than to Rationall. . . .
> But when the words Free, and Liberty, are applyed to any thing but Bodies, they are abused; for that which is not subject to Motion, is not subject to Impediment. . . .[9]

According to Hobbes, a river is free to run in its channel in just the same way that a man is free to pay his debts. Hobbes's materialist account of freedom is bound up with his materialist ontology in general. Even God and the soul are described in *Leviathan* as very subtle forms of matter.

The univocal application of "freedom" in Hobbes's sense to persons and objects is an indication of the difficulties of his account. Surely the freedom of a person to act is something distinct from the "freedom"— if we may even use the word—of water to run in its channel.

Indeed, Hobbes's definition is both too inclusive and too stringent. First, not every external impediment to motion diminishes a person's freedom to act. The presence of a steep mountain range may prevent a person from travelling from one valley to another, but it does not deprive him of the freedom to do so. He is free to pass over the mountains, provided he is able to find a route.

Second, many influences which are not physical obstacles are genuine restrictions on freedom. For persons act in ways that objects do not, and their behavior can be affected in ways that cannot be applied to bodies. A gunman who demands that a river change its course will find his threats ineffectual, but if he demands money from travellers on the river he will get it. And in threatening the travellers, even though he imposes on them no physical impediment to motion (until he actually fires his gun and physically harms them), he diminishes their freedom. It is above all the interference of other persons which restricts freedom, and the interference need not include physical restraint.

Hobbes denies that threats interfere with freedom, since they do not impede motion. On Hobbes's account, a threatened penalty leaves an agent no less free than he was without the threat.

> Feare and Liberty are consistent; as when a man throweth his goods into the Sea for feare the Ship should sink, he doth it very willingly, and may refuse to doe it if he will: It is therefore the action, of one that was free: so a man sometimes pays his debt, only for feare of Imprisonment, which because no body hindred him from detaining, was the action of a man at liberty. And generally all actions which men doe in Commonwealths, for feare of the law, [are] actions, which the doers had liberty to omit.[10]

But Hobbes's account is clearly unsatisfactory. Acting in response to a coercive threat is not acting freely. The threat of intolerable consequences deprives a person of freedom just as effectively as does the infliction of physical force. Only those "external impediments to motion" which are imposed by other persons diminish freedom; and, on the other hand, freedom may be just as effectively destroyed or limited by other kinds of interference.

Absence of Interference by Others

With these considerations in mind, a number of recent writers have defined freedom as precisely the absence of interference by other persons with the determination of an individual's actions by his will. Thus Isaiah Berlin in "Two Concepts of Liberty":

> I am normally said to be free to the extent to which no man or body of men interferes with my activity. Political liberty in this sense is simply the area within which a man can act unobstructed by others. . . . You lack political liberty or freedom only if you are prevented from attaining a goal by human beings.[11]

Similarly, F. A. Hayek in *The Constitution of Liberty* defines "freedom" as "the state in which a man is not subject to coercion by the arbitrary will of another or others."[12]

Berlin and Hayek agree that it is interference by persons and not by physical conditions that restricts freedom. Hayek states that

> "freedom" refers solely to a relation of men to other men, and the only infringement on it is coercion by men. The range of physical possibilities open to a person has no relevance to freedom: The rock climber on a difficult pitch who sees only one way out to save his life is unquestionably free, though we would hardly say he has any choice.[13]

Berlin's understanding of liberty is similar, and—although he describes liberty in this sense only as "political liberty"—he regards absence of interference by others as central to the concept of liberty.

Hayek's claim that freedom is infringed only by others' coercion is clearly too strong, for there are other kinds of interference that have a similar effect on freedom. Physical compulsion deprives the individual of freedom to act. Noncoercive duress, and the removal of alternatives, do not destroy but nevertheless diminish or limit freedom. Let us take Berlin's more general statement as a formulation of this third major conception of freedom: a person is free to the extent that no one else interferes with her activity. Freedom is the absence of interference by other persons.

It is clear, I think, that this account strikes closer to the truth than either the Lockean view of freedom as acting as one will or the Hobbesian definition of freedom as the absence of impediment to motion. Both of those accounts mistakenly include factors and conditions which we do not count as rendering agents unfree—inabilities in the former case, physical circumstances in the latter—as infringements of freedom. Hobbes's definition also fails to count coercion as a restriction on freedom. The definition of freedom as the absence of others' interference seems to classify these obstacles to freedom correctly.

Yet this third account of freedom still excludes too much. To be sure, we do not usually think of a mountain range as making the residents of a valley unfree. And yet can it not be said that the automobile and the airplane have greatly extended our freedom to travel? If freedom means lack of interference, this is a senseless claim. The removal of a coercive threat greatly increases my freedom; but so does an airline pass or a check for $100,000. And so might a program of counseling which freed me from neurotic fears.

The Berlin-Hayek account of freedom must either describe all such cases circuitously, as removal of some peculiar kind of interference by others, or label them as misuses or metaphorical uses of the term "freedom." The reason why these writers count acts of interference by others as infringements of freedom is clear: these are acts which we recognize as restrictions on freedom, and they are among the most important limits on freedom which interaction in society imposes. But this is no reason to count *only* such interference as restricting freedom and to relegate the examples just mentioned to the category of misuse or metaphor.

Freedom and Freedoms

All three of the accounts of freedom discussed above have taken *freedom* to be a single, univocal term; they have spoken of freedom in general rather than of specific freedoms. Perhaps the relation between freedom and coercion can be clearly discerned only if we specify with greater precision just what freedom, or what kind of freedom, we are speaking of.

Gerald MacCallum has argued that freedom is a triadic relation among persons, things, and actions: Freedom is always freedom *of* someone *from* something *to* do or become something. Implicit in every assertion of freedom, MacCallum argues, is something like the following formula: "x is free from y to do or become z," where x ranges over agents, y over constraints, restrictions, interferences, or barriers, and z

over actions or conditions of character.[14] One or more variables in this formula may frequently be left unspecified, to be inferred from the context of the discussion. Disputes over the meaning of the term "freedom," MacCallum argues, actually employ the term in just the same sense but give different accounts of the ranges of the variables.

In this light, the Lockean and Hobbesian accounts of freedom can be seen to be incomplete rather than altogether misguided. Locke concentrated on freedom of agents to do as they will, but he failed to distinguish among several importantly different kinds of constraints. Hobbes identified freedom with absence of one kind of constraint, viz. physical impediment. Berlin and Hayek identify freedom with the absence of another kind of constraint, interference by others. All three of the latter writers have made the category of limits to freedom overly narrow and have failed to specify what it is that we want to be free to do.

The truth is that we may speak of freedom and unfreedom in all of these ways. We do not normally count a mountain as limiting freedom. But we might say, "The roads are clear now through the pass, so you are free to take this route." The freedom here invoked is freedom from physical impediments to travel along a certain route. Similarly, although inability is not lack of freedom, we might say that we have gained new freedom by overcoming certain inabilities, and we frequently speak of "freeing ourselves" from states such as worry and fear. In such cases we are speaking of freedom from internal obstacles to acting as we choose.

Any attempt to specify precisely what sorts of obstacles and restraints should be taken as limits on freedom, then, will be to a certain extent arbitrary. Under appropriate circumstances, any number of conditions, states, and actions may be taken as constraints on freedom, as values for y in the formula above. These include not only actions of other agents but physical circumstances, internal states, social conditions, and the like.

But even though we can speak of freedom from any number of kinds of obstacles and constraints, they are not all of equal concern to us. In considering the effects of social structures on freedom, in particular, some limits on freedom are of greater relevance and importance than others. And here is the truth of the definition of freedom as absence of interference: among the many obstacles to freedom of agents to act as they will, interference by other agents is of particular concern to us in constructing and evaluating social institutions.

MacCallum appears willing to count any hindrance to action as a restriction on freedom. A more cautious conclusion from the cases I have mentioned above is that there is no general category of obstacles to action which can never be counted as restricting freedom. For any category we choose—physical features of the environment, internal conditions, even inabilities—we can find circumstances in which something of this kind would count as limiting an agent's freedom. Attempts to distinguish limits on freedom from other obstacles by identifying relevant categories of obstacles, therefore, are bound to fail. This more modest conclusion does not commit us to the implausible claim that, for example, human beings are unfree to fly or to leap tall buildings in a single bound. Possibly there are circumstances in which we would speak of such inabilities as limits on freedom, but in normal discourse we do not.

Freedom in General

The broadening of the concept of freedom which MacCallum proposes does not resolve the problem of what constitutes freedom but simply relocates it. Consider the difference between freedom from coercion and violence, on the one hand, and freedom from earthquakes and avalanches, on the other. The former, clearly, is a freedom which is of central concern to us in political contexts, while the latter usually is not. Hayek and Berlin assert that the latter is not freedom in the proper sense at all, since the ill from which we are said to be free is not the intervention of other persons; but this requires an arbitrary and unsupported limitation on what counts as a restriction of freedom. On MacCallum's account, both of these constitute freedom in the proper sense—freedom of someone from something to do something. But we must now face the further question of why certain restrictions on freedom are of greater concern to us than others. To put the matter differently, MacCallum has given a plausible account of the various kinds of freedom, but we still need an account of what restraints and what actions are implicitly referred to when we speak in general of a person's being free.

The answer would seem to be that when we speak nonspecifically about freedom we have in mind, on the one hand, a class of constraints which we are normally concerned to avoid and, on the other, a class of actions of the kinds which we might normally intend. To say that "Barbara is free," in other words, is to say that unfreedoms of the kind that we are concerned to escape do not hinder her from doing any of the things we might normally expect her to want to do.

Despite the difficulty of identifying just what falls into the range of "normal" constraints and actions, an account of this kind enables us to apply MacCallum's triadic analysis to the examples of freedom and unfreedom that have been mentioned. We do not count lack of wings as restricting a person's freedom, for example, because we do not normally expect flying to be one of the things that human beings want or attempt to do. We need a further description of unusual circumstances to persuade us that this hindrance limits freedom. Perhaps a wingless person among a race of winged humanoids is unfree to fly.

When we speak of freedom *tout court* we implicitly invoke a class of obstacles to freedom that we are free from and a range of actions that we are free to do. Both are determined in part by the particular context of use and in part by general assumptions about what a person is concerned to be free from and may want to do. Being able to move about freely is something which is important to nearly all persons, and therefore any restriction on our movements diminishes our freedom. But the closing off of certain alternatives which no one is likely even to think about doing does not count as a restriction, or at any rate as a significant restriction, on our freedom. Erecting a fence around a nuclear waste disposal site is an example: the fence prevents me from walking about the site, but since no one wants to expose himself to dangerous radiation, this restriction on freedom of movement does not make me signficantly less free.

We normally care only about alternatives that *might* be open to us, things that we could do if certain obstacles were absent. No one bemoans his lack of the freedom to trisect angles or to move mountains with his bare hands. Among the actions we are free or unfree to do we count only those that we are able, logically and physically, to do.

The hindrances that we count as obstacles to freedom, moreover, compose a subclass of the obstacles that are alterable by human action. To be free *tout court* is to be free from those hindrances to action which could be removed by others' actions. And although a great many obstacles *can* be removed by human effort, it is the interference of other agents with our acting as we will that is of particular concern to us when we speak of freedom in general.

Ther are several reasons why, among all the potential obstacles to our free action, we place particular importance on absence of others' interference. First, interference greatly reduces the number of alternatives available to us. Coercion, for example, does not merely rule out a few of our previous choices but leaves only one reasonable alternative open. It is therefore a severe restriction on the range of our choice. Second, these unfreedoms, unlike others, are directly tied to others' acts. All that is necessary to remove these obstacles is for others to refrain from certain actions.

Third, and perhaps most important, interference carries with it a sense of personal injury or affront by subordinating the victim to the will of another. A fire and a coercive threat may just as effectively limit my choices, but only the latter carries with it the personal offense of being manipulated by another.

There are other limits on freedom which may be equally severe. A paralyzing stroke leaves its victim very few alternatives, for example; it limits freedom, perhaps, even more drastically than does coercion. On the other hand, there are other kinds of unfreedom besides the interference of others which are also avoidable. Physical obstacles to action, including not only disease but geographical and climatic conditions, can be removed or at least ameliorated through concerted human effort. A technologically advanced society can undertake, for example, to provide its members freedom to move about unimpeded by mountain ranges or floods.

But to rank these as more serious infringements of freedom than others' interference would be a misjudgment of priorities. Both the context of discourse and the undesirability of interference require the reverse ranking. First, interference by other persons is more readily removed or diminished by concerted social action than are either physical limits or internal incapacities, and for that reason it is more relevant to the design and assessment of social institutions. Second, while we are willing to accept and make adjustments for physical and psychological inabilities and obstacles, coercion and violence divert us radically from the expected course of events in an unpredictable and highly undesirable way.

For both of these reasons, when we assess the extent of a person's freedom in a society, our principal concern is with the person's freedom from others' interference. Obstacles to freedom such as physical conditions and geographic barriers are not usually counted as infringements of freedom precisely because they are normal, expected, and relatively unchanging aspects of our world. Coercion and violence inflicted by others, on the other hand—even if they occur frequently—lack this quality of normality, and when we speak of freedom without qualification we have in mind such freedom especially.

We can imagine a society which leaves its members open to theft, fraud, assault, and the like but which bends all of its efforts and resources to preventing floods, building good roads through mountain passes, and helping individuals overcome psychological impairments.[15] Few would deny, however, that such a society would be neglecting the unfreedom which ought to be among its primary concerns: social institutions ought, whatever else they may undertake, to try to free individuals from unwanted forceful interference.

I shall return in the following chapter to the reasons for the priority we attach to freedom from interference. Each person, it will be argued, has a right to be free from interference by others with his making and carrying out choices. It is not that such freedom must always take priority over other kinds of freedom or over all other desired ends. To attach an absolute or "lexicographical" priority to others' interference over all else would be too strong a claim. The claim I am here defending is rather the more modest assertion that freedom from interference—from coercion, violence, and the like—is a central element in the general and unspecific notion of social freedom.

In summary, there are many kinds of circumstances and influences which can be counted as diminishing freedom. These should be accommodated not by ruling all but certain class out by definitional fiat but by recognizing that *any* hindrance to an agent's doing something *may* limit his freedom, whether the hindrance comes from another agent's action, from physical events and circumstances, or from the agent's own desires, intentions, or psychological state. This does not imply, however, that all unfreedoms are of equal importance, particularly in considering the nature and structure of social institutions. When we speak of freedom we have in mind a range of actions which an agent might want to do and a range of obstacles to doing them. In a political context, coercion is one of the principal obstacles to a person's freedom because it is one that is seldom predictable, carries a sense of personal affront, and is avoidable through concerted social action.

There is no limit to the kinds of obstacles that may limit freedom. A person's freedom may be diminished by another's act or failure to act, by a physical object or by the lack of some physical object (a tool or a car), by the *Zeitgeist* or by the weather. In assessing social institutions, however, it is others' interference that is of primary concern, and when we speak of freedom in political contexts, it is this freedom above all that we mean. Berlin and Hayek are wrong in using the term "freedom" of this kind of freedom alone, but they point correctly to the central meaning of freedom for political philosophy.

Are Coerced Acts Free?

The question with which we began our discussion of coercion was whether a coerced act is done freely, and I began by pointing to the apparent inconsistency that we count coercion as a paradigm example of lack of freedom even though the victim of coercion acts voluntarily. None of the definitions of freedom discussed offers a fully satisfactory account of this puzzle. Locke seems to say that whether the victim of coercion is free depends on what he would antecedently have wanted to do. Hobbes baldly asserts that coercion is not a constraint on freedom. Berlin and Hayek count coercion as an example of unfreedom simply by defining freedom arbitrarily as the absence of force or coercion. MacCallum's analysis of freedom would have us break down the general question, "Is the victim of coercion free?", into two questions: "Is he free from physical compulsion to keep his money?", for example, and "Is he free from the threat of force to keep his money?" In a genuine instance of coercion the answer to the first question will be "yes" and that to the second question "no." This helps, perhaps, to clarify our question about the effect of coercion on freedom; but it does not even begin to answer it. For our concern was with freedom in a more general sense, which I have described as freedom from unexpected and unwanted hindrances to doing the kinds of things that persons normally want to do.

We can distill from this broad notion of freedom two narrower notions that will help make the effect of coercion on freedom clearer, however. What the victim of coercion is able to do despite the threat is to control his actions in the usual way. His control over the movements of his own body has not been taken from him, as it is in cases of compulsion. He is free from physical restraint to act as he wills; in short, he is *free to act*.

What has been taken from the victim of coercion is the ability to determine his future condition by his actions, to bring about future conditions which he desires by his present acts. Of course, his acts still determine in part what his future condition will be; but the normal control that we have and expect over what happens to us as a result of our actions has been disrupted by the threat. The victim of coercion, then, is subjected to extraordinary constraints on his choice; in short, he is not *free to choose*.

Distinguishing these two senses of freedom makes possible a clearer statement of the effect of coercion on freedom and of the difference between coercion and other means of influencing behavior. The victim of coercion is free to act but not free to choose; he has the normal sort of control over his bodily actions but lacks the normal kinds of control over his choices and their consequences. Compulsion, in contrast, leaves its victim neither freedom of action nor freedom of choice. Persuasion, at the other extreme, preserves freedom of both kinds.

Notes

1. See, for example, Isaiah Berlin, "Two Concepts of Liberty," in *Four Essays on Liberty* (New York: Oxford University Press, 1969), 121.

2. John Locke, *Essay Concerning Human Understanding*, bk. 1, chap. 21, para. 8; ed. Alexander C. Fraser (New York: Dover, 1959), 1:316. In subsequent references to this work the volume and page number in the Fraser edition are given in parentheses.

3. Locke, *Essay*, 1. 21. 21 (1:325).

4. Locke, *Essay*, 1. 21. 10 (1:317).

5. Haskell Fain, "Prediction and Constraint," *Mind* 67 (1958): 372.

6. A person may want at the same time to do several mutually exclusive things: she may want to study, to go bicycling, and to meet her friends at a tavern. Only one of these desires can be satisfied at one time (unless there is a Bicycle Book Bar nearby). Depending on the strength of the relevant desires, she must decide to fulfill one of these desires, or to do something else altogether. Her *will* can follow only one of her conflicting desires.

It is also possible to want to do several things, or to desire several conditions, which are not merely in temporal conflict but incompatible. A person may want to be both a good jockey and a prizewinning heavyweight boxer, even though the diet and physical training which would bring about the former would render him unfit for the latter. Desires may even involve logically inconsistent ends. A person may want, for such and such reasons, to be twenty pounds heavier and also want, for different reasons, to be twenty pounds lighter. (Possibly even partly for the same reasons, e.g., that he is tired of his present wardrobe and wants a compelling reason to replace it.)

But it is not possible to *will* incompatible or inconsistent states or actions. No one can decide to become a successful jockey and a first-rate heavyweight fighter at the same time. A person may will to gain or to lose weight but not to do both at once.

7. Thomas Hobbes, *Leviathan* (1651), pt. 1, chap. 14; ed. C. B. MacPherson (Baltimore: Penguin Books, 1968), 189; ed. Michael Oakeshott (Oxford: Blackwell, 1960), 84. Subsequent references will be to the MacPherson edition, with page numbers in the Oakeshott edition given in parentheses. I follow MacPherson rather than Oakeshott in retaining Hobbes's spelling and punctuation.

8. Hobbes, *Leviathan*, 262 (137).

9. Hobbes, *Leviathan*, 261–62 (136–37).

10. Hobbes, *Leviathan*, 262–63 (137).

11. Berlin, *Four Essays on Liberty*, 122.

12. F. A. Hayek, *The Constitution of Liberty* (Chicago: University of Chicago Press, 1960), 11.

13. Hayek, *Constitution of Liberty*, 12.

14. Gerald MacCallum, "Positive and Negative Freedom," *Philosophical Review*, 76, no. 3 (July 1967): 314. A similar account of freedom is given by Felix Oppenheim in *Dimensions of Freedom* (New York: St. Martin's Press, 1961).

15. I am assuming that not all theft, fraud, and assault are the result of psychological malfunctions. More on this in chapter 6, below.

6
THE PLACE OF RIGHTS
IN MORAL JUDGMENT

Our concern thus far has been primarily with the nature of coercion itself—with the features which distinguish it from other means of interpersonal influence and with the connection between coercion and questions of freedom and responsibility. It is time now to turn to issues which are more directly involved in the moral judgments which we make concerning coercive actions and institutions. The present chapter and the next will ground a general account of the justifiability of coercion in a theory concerning the nature and force of rights. The chapters which follow, and which will close our study, explore the application of this general account, and of the analysis of coercion which has already been provided, to some specific areas in which coercion is applied. Institutions of punishment will be examined as an extended test of the theory of coercion which is put forward in this study.

The present chapter is devoted to an account of the nature of rights and of the place of rights in the moral assessment of actions. I will argue in favor of an ethical theory which takes human or natural rights as a fundamental category of moral evaluation, and, in the chapter following, I will argue that recognition of human rights gives rise to two general judgments about coercion. First, there is a moral presumption against coercion—its use is *prima facie* wrong—because coercion violates the right of persons to self-determination. Second, a proper understanding of the nature of rights shows that coercion is justified in certain circumstances in which rights have been or are judged likely to be violated, because human rights include second-order rights to protect the exercise of rights when necessary.

Why Rights?

The concept of a right is one of a small number of basic moral concepts. Ronald Dworkin has distinguished *goals*, *rights*, and *duties* as the fundamental justifying devices in political theories and has suggested that any theory will make one of these the category which ultimately grounds all judgments about the justification of political decisions or institutions.[1]

The account I offer of the moral status of coercion will be built primarily on the category of rights. Why should this particular category be taken as fundamental—and would the choice of a different starting point lead to significantly different conclusions about the justifiability of coercion? Before proceeding with our account of coercion and its relation to rights we need to face these questions of moral theory.

It might be possible to construct a political theory on the basis of duties, such as the duty to be fair. I am not aware of any political philosopher who has done so, however; and the principal competitors to rights-based political theories in Western thought have been consequentialist ethical theories, theories which count the achievement of certain goals as the basic criterion of moral worth and value.[2] I shall explore in this section the ways in which a political theory based on goals would differ from a rights-based theory in its treatment of coercion.

I have chosen to take rights as the normative basis for my account of coercion for two reasons. First, coercion is an area in which moral judgments based on rights have a clear application, and it is an area in which we frequently invoke rights to criticize others' actions. An account of coercion based on rights preserves this link. Because coercion is tied to rights in our common moral judgments, an account of coercion based on rights is less apt than is a consequentialist account to lead to counterintuitive conclusions or to judgments which we would find questionable. Second, a theory based on natural rights is in some ways conceptually simpler than a consequentialist theory: the moral status of coercion emerges more clearly and more simply from a rights-based theory than from one based on goals.

Neither of these, I recognize, is a conclusive argument in favor of a rights-based ethical theory. It may be that the way we commonly speak of coercion and its moral status is wrong; and it is possible that the ethical account of this issue which is conceptually simplest is for some other reason ill-conceived or poorly grounded. I do not believe that is the case, however, and I will argue that the particular natural or human rights I invoke in assessing the moral standing of coercion are rights which have a firm basis in the way that we treat and conceive of persons.

I make no claim to offer irrefutable grounds for placing rights rather than goals at the basis of moral judgment, for I do not believe that any such categorical judgment is defensible. The rights-based account which I offer seems to me to be a more satisfactory account of coercion than any alternative based on goals. But a great deal depends on the particular character of the theories in question, and doubtless there are consequentialist ethical theories which are preferable, perhaps on the very grounds I have mentioned, to certain kinds of rights-based or deontological theories. Moreover, the difference between the two kinds of theories should not be exaggerated. Their disagreement concerning the basic ground and source of moral judgments is fundamental; and yet an emphasis on rights as the basis of morality does not entail that consequential matters are morally irrelevant, or vice versa. In particular, even a basically deontological theory must allow that the end brought about by an action frequently has an important place in moral judgment.

So the question is not really whether goals are morally relevant. Unquestionably they are. The question that must be faced is rather whether goals provide a sufficient basis for moral evaluation. Must a moral theory in which reference is not made to individual rights, or in which talk about rights is taken to refer elliptically to actions which bring about certain kinds of ends, lead to significantly different—and less acceptable—moral judgments, in particular cases, than a theory which gives rights priority?

The answer to this question, I believe, is that whether the judgments differ depends on which goals are taken as morally basic and on how their achievement is assessed. A utilitarian moral theory, to take the most familiar form of consequentialism in moral theory, will lead to very different and morally unacceptable results. A nonutilitarian consequentialist theory, however, may yield judgments very similar to those of a rights-based theory.

According to the utilitarian version of goal-based ethics, whether an action is right or wrong depends entirely on the quantitative goodness of the consequences which it brings about or is judged likely to bring about. Bentham and Mill described the goodness of consequences in terms of the happiness or utility caused all persons affected by the action.[3] Recent defenders of utilitarianism, recognizing the difficulty of summing the happiness of all agents into a single composite quantity, have spoken more generally of right actions as actions which bring about the greatest degree of satisfaction of the desires of all persons affected. Whatever explanation of the measurement of the good may be given, utilitarians are agreed that nothing except the goodness of consequences is relevant to moral evaluation. Individual rights ought to be recognized, therefore, if and only if doing so will lead in the long run to the greatest net balance of good over evil consequences.

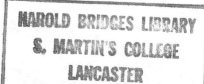

The debate over the adequacy of a utilitarian system of ethics has been long and complex, and I cannot attempt to trace its progress in detail here.[4] I shall instead consider a specific example of a situation in which the inadequacy of utilitarianism, and especially its undervaluation of individual rights, can be plainly seen.

Suppose that a small group of people in a society hold a particular political viewpoint which the rest of the members of the society find repugnant. The small group are fanatic defenders of their view. They proclaim it on street corners, erect billboards, stage frequent parades, and the like, all of which causes distress and unhappiness to everyone else. It is evident that, within the legal and moral framework of modern Western societies, we are firmly committed to the judgment that such a minority should be allowed to present its views freely, subject only to necessary restrictions which protect the rights of others. They may hold parades on Saturday afternoon but not in the wee hours of Sunday morning, for example; they may display their posters freely but may not glue them onto other people's houses. To permit these practices, however, plainly diminishes the overall happiness of the members of society, since—as we have described the example—the offending group has very few members, and the offense and distress which they cause others are keenly felt and deeply resented. In this case, therefore, utilitarian considerations would not only permit but require that the group be prevented from presenting their views.

A utilitarian might argue that such circumstances will in fact never arise. It is difficult to know how to assess the truth of such an empirical claim; but in any case this response does not answer the legitimate question of what we ought to do if, contrary to all expectations, we found ourselves in such a situation. The utilitarian position might also be defended by arguing, as Mill does in *On Liberty*, that free expression of opinion must always lead to the greatest quantity of good in the long run.[5] But such a response is likely to rest—as Mill's position does, I believe—on implausible empirical assumptions about the utility of truth and its inevitable triumph over falsehood. If we set aside any such empirical claims, Mill's position seems to lead unavoidably to the invocation of nonutilitarian moral considerations about the importance of individual expression. For if, no matter how small the offending group and how great the offense, the free expression of opinion outweighs all else, then moral judgments cannot rest solely on consequences.

A strict utilitarian cannot meet this objection convincingly without either tempering his commitment to a single standard of goodness or departing decisively from a widely shared moral judgment. The objection might be met, however, by a system of ethics which, while still broadly consequentialist, allows for differing degrees of importance or urgency among desires and ends.[6] It might be argued that the desire of the majority to avoid hearing doctrines repugnant to them is a desire of less importance than the desire of the minority to proclaim their view, or that the former want or need is less urgent than the latter.

A consequentialist account of political judgments which differentiates between degrees of urgency or importance does seem able to deal with conflicting desires in a more satisfactory way than can a strictly utilitarian theory. Even if rights are not themselves taken as fundamental, it may be said that the satisfaction of the most urgent desires takes precedence even over a considerably greater quantity of satisfaction of less urgent desires. Ranking of this kind can bear much of the weight which I will place in the account below on the rights of individuals.

Such a broadly consequentialist view regards measurement of the good consequences of an action or institution as only the first step toward its moral evaluation. The satisfaction of desires must be weighted according to the comparative importance of the desires or needs which are fulfilled. Such a theory gains a greater fidelity to our moral judgments at the cost of giving up the conceptual simplicity of utilitarianism, for the difficult problem of identifying the relations of priority and urgency among desires and needs remains. The problem of determining which are the most urgent interests, moreover, does not seem substantially less difficult than the parallel problem which a rights-based theory faces in identifying the rights of individuals. I employ the concept of rights as the basis for the moral assessment of coercion, therefore, not because only such a theory can yield acceptable judgments about coercion but because no alternative theory seems preferable on grounds either of simplicity or of fidelity to moral judgments that we share. Furthermore, the concept of rights is closely intertwined with our moral judgments about coercive institutions, and analysis of rights will illuminate both the presumption against and the defense of coercion.

The Nature of Rights

Because the analysis of the moral status of coercion which I will offer is based largely on an account of rights, it is important to identify as clearly as possible what a right is. In this section, therefore, I offer an account of what it means to assert that a person has a right. The definition I offer will be expanded and put to use in the following chapter to show that rights offer a moral basis on which coercion can be justified.

In his 1923 study of *Fundamental Legal Conceptions* Wesley Hohfeld distinguished four senses in which a person may have a legal right. First, there are rights in the strict sense, which are correlative with duties: "In other words, if X has a right against Y that he shall stay off the former's land, the correlative (and equivalent) is that Y is under a duty toward X to stay off the place."[7] A second category is that of *privileges* or liberties, which are the negations of duties. In the example just cited, "whereas X has a *right* or *claim* that Y, the other man, should stay off the land, he himself has the *privilege* of entering on the land; or, in other words, X does not have a duty to stay off."[8] Correlatively, another person has no right to demand that the owner stay off the land; Hohfeld acknowledges that there is no established term for this legal status and refers to it as a "no-right."

The third and fourth categories have to do with the voluntary acts by which one person can change another's legal status. A *power* is the legal ability to bring about a change in the legal relations between the person who holds the power and another. An example is the power of the owner of property to dissolve his legal interests in his property through abandonment.[9] Correlative to a power is the liability of others to have their legal relations changed through its exercise. Finally, an *immunity* is the negation of a liability: it consists in "freedom from the legal power or control of another as regards some legal relation."[10] The correlative relation of others is the legal disability to exercise certain powers. Immunity of certain corporations or charitable institutions from taxation is an example.

Legal rights commonly include several of these elements. Property rights, for example, include the liberty to use one's property, the claim against others that they not use it without permission, and the power to transfer ownership. If the property is held as a homestead, the property right also includes immunity against its seizure by creditors.

Hohfeld's account is a description of rights in law, and the rights he discusses exist only as defined in a legal system. Since our purpose here is to subject legal systems themselves to critical evaluation and to determine when coercion is justifiably or illegitimately used by governmental institutions, his account can provide only a starting point. We must pursue the analysis of rights to the level of moral or human rights.

Hohfeld argues that each category of legal right includes or implies a correlative legal status of persons with respect to whom the right is held. This feature of rights is equally characteristic of moral rights in nonlegal contexts. Stanley Benn interprets Hohfeld's account of rights and correlatives to imply that the relation between the two is one of identity. On Benn's account, one person's claim-right is the same as another's duty, considered from a different perspective.[11] Benn and Peters assert that the connection between right and duty, in moral as well as legal contexts, is not moral but logical: the existence of a duty entails the existence of a right in those to whom a duty is owed.[12]

But this is too strong a claim. We have a duty to act benevolently toward others, for example, but no one has a right to our benevolent action. Or, to take a different kind of example: Kant argued that persons have duties toward themselves. Even those who deny that there are such duties understand what duties are being asserted by their defenders.[13] But if the relation between right and duty were one of identity or logical entailment, these duties would be identical with or entail rights held with respect to oneself. And the latter, surely, is an incoherent notion.

Duties, then, cannot be identical with rights, for there are duties without corresponding rights. There are no rights, however, without corresponding duties. The connection between these concepts—though it is misleading to call it identity—may yet be a logical one. That you have property rights to a certain piece of land is all I need to know in order to draw the conclusion that I ought to stay off it without your permission. The duty is entailed by, or is a part of, the right.

This connection does not hold for what Hohfeld calls liberties. There is no commonly identified legal status correlative to such rights. Hohfeld, as we have noted, invents the term "no-right" to refer to the absence of an obligation. This might be taken as evidence that rights do not always entail corresponding duties; but it is more plausibly taken instead as evidence that liberties are not rights in the proper sense. In any case, whatever may be the nonlegal analogue of having a liberty and no stronger right, such moral permissions are of little importance for the assessment and adjudication of rights.[14] In the remainder of this discussion, therefore, I shall disregard the second of Hohfeld's four senses of "right" and consider only what he calls claim-rights, powers, and immunities.

The character of moral rights is different in several respects from that of legal rights, and if we try to apply Hohfeld's account to nonlegal rights it proves insufficient. It is the availability of legal recourse for violation, for example, that distinguishes claim-rights from liberties; but no such institutional recourse supports moral rights.[15] Powers and immunities are rights which operate at a further remove from actions than do claim-rights, since they have to do with the conditions under which actions count as legally significant and as altering the legal status of future actions.[16] There do not seem to be precisely corresponding nonlegal categories—it is not obvious what would count as a moral power or a moral immunity, for example, although it is possible to create duties and to affect the moral character of future actions through voluntary actions such as promising and marrying.

The correlative duties created by moral rights are of two significantly different kinds. Some rights, such as the right to free practice of one's religion or to freedom of movement, impose on others a negative duty, a duty to refrain from interfering with the exercise of the right. Such rights create in other persons a duty not to do anything which impedes the exercise of the right. In contrast, other rights, such as the right to an adequate diet or to an education, impose a positive duty on others to contribute to the securing of the right. Persons who hold such rights may claim as their right not merely that others stand out of the way and allow them the exercise of their right but that others actively support them in achieving what they have a right to.

Every right is held by some person or persons with respect to others. We may accordingly distinguish among moral rights by asking who holds the right with respect to whom. Some rights, in Hart's terminology, are *special rights*, rights which arise from transactions or special relationships, such as the power of attorney or permission to use property. The duties created by special rights fall only on the others involved in the act or relationship from which the right arises. Other rights are *general rights*, held by one person with respect to all others, such as the right to freedom of speech.[17] Both special and general rights may be held by some individuals and not by others, or they may be held by all.

Among moral rights, or rights in nonlegal contexts, we can draw distinctions similar to those Hohfeld draws among legal rights. We may note first the existence of moral liberties or permissions. There are actions which we are morally permitted to do concerning which others have no corresponding duties either to refrain from impeding or to assist us. Examples might include the liberty to enter into agreements or the liberty to sell a product for a certain price. We are morally entitled to do these things, but if someone else interferes with our doing so—if another merchant sells similar products for a lower price, for example, and thus prevents us from getting the price we wanted—no rights of ours have been infringed. Because this is the case I shall not refer to moral liberties as rights; they provide no basis for moral claims against others, and therefore the word "right" seems too strong to describe them.[18]

Moral rights in the proper sense create corresponding duties, which may be duties of noninterference or duties of contribution. Duties of nonintervention are conditional duties: they are duties to refrain from interfering with a person's exercise of her right, and the duty not to interfere is conditional on the right-holder's performance of the kinds of acts which she has a right to do.[19] But the duty of noninterference makes unconditional demands also: I may not take away the means of exercising a right, even if the holder of the right shows no interest in exercising it.

Duties of contribution may be either conditional or unconditional. If A has a right to an adequate diet, then B's correlative duty may be either a duty to contribute to A's welfare when A asks him to or an unconditional duty to contribute. It seems likely that all duties of contribution are conditional duties, conditional on either a request or an evident need for assistance. (If I find a starving person by the roadside, too weak to speak, I may not wait to see whether he manages to croak, "Food, please," to determine whether I have a duty to assist him.) But there may also be unconditional duties to contribute.

An important class of rights is comprised by rights *not* to have certain things done to one—the right not to be assaulted and the right not to be arrested without warrant, for example. These are similar to rights to engage in certain kinds of activity without interference, but the specificity is on the other side. The right to vote, for example, is a right to engage in a certain activity, which we can specify with great precision, and to be free from interference of any kind with one's doing so. The right not be assaulted, in contrast, is a right to engage in whatever activity one may choose and to be free in doing so from one specific kind of interference.

The observations that have been made about the nature and kinds of moral rights may be summed up in a compound definition. Where X and Y are persons and A is an activity or object, we may speak of rights in any of the following senses:

(R1) X has a right$_1$ to A over against Y just in case X is at liberty with respect to A and for this reason Y has a duty not to interfere with X's doing or having A.

(R2) X has a right$_2$ not to suffer A over against Y just in case Y has a duty not to do A to X.[20]

(R3) X has a right$_3$ to A over against Y just in case X is at liberty with respect to A and Y has a duty not to refuse to assist X in doing or having A.

(R4) X has a right$_4$ to A over against Y just in case X is at liberty with respect to A and Y has a duty to assist X in doing or having A.

To say that X is at liberty with respect to an activity or object is to say that it is morally permissible for him to engage in the activity or to possess the object. The role of rights in moral judgments is to provide a defense for an individual's actions: an action may be shown to be morally permissible by showing that in doing the action the agent exercises a right. But the moral defense provided by a right is by no means always conclusive. It is sometimes morally wrong to exercise a right. Others' rights, or other moral considerations, may override a right and disallow its exercise. To seize a boat in order to rescue someone from drowning is to infringe on the property rights of the boat's owner, and yet the owner would be wrong to insist on his property rights under such circumstances.

Particular moral rights may be of any of these kinds or may involve rights in several of the senses listed. Property rights—considered as moral rights, not as part of a legal system—include the $right_1$ to exclusive use of one's property and the $right_2$ that others not trespass on it, as well as the liberty to use the property as one chooses. The right to receive one's inheritance, if such a right exists, is a $right_3$ or $right_4$ held by one person with respect to certain others—his parents or other relatives—that they perform a certain action, and it also includes a $right_1$ with respect to all others that he be permitted to receive what is due him without their interference. Such a right would be infringed not only if the executors of the parents' estate refuse to give the holder his share but also if a confiscatory tax is imposed on bequests. $Rights_1$ and $rights_2$ overlap considerably: rights such as freedom of speech and freedom of the person are rights to engage in certain kinds of activity and to be free in doing so from certain kinds of interference. Welfare rights might be described as either $rights_3$ or $rights_4$, and they are perhaps the most likely candidates for $rights_4$, which create an unconditional duty to contribute.[21]

The various kinds of rights can be illustrated by the example of a race. Anyone who enters a race has a $right_1$ to compete fairly, and there is a correlative duty of other competitors and observers not to interfere by unfair means. We might also describe this right, or a part of it, by saying that each contestant has a $right_2$ not to be tripped, elbowed, or the like in the course of the race. Each contestant also has the liberty to win: she has no duty to refrain from winning, but her liberty is less than a right because it imposes no duty on others either to assist her or to stand by and allow her to win. No one in a race, however, has a $right_3$ or a $right_4$ either to compete or to win.

The features so far identified are features widely recognized as elements of the concept of rights, and the account I have offered is similar to several others.[22] There is another feature of rights, however, which has received little attention. A distinctive feature of rights among moral concepts is the *appropriateness of force or coercion* to ensure their recognition.[23] Few would recommend, for example, that the moral duty to show kindness be backed by the use or threat of force. The suggestion seems inappropriate or incongruous. But there is no such incongruity in the suggestion that the rights of persons should be protected by forceful means if necessary. Rights are frequently asserted as a justification for the use of force.

In Chapter Eight, below, we will return to the topic of the place of force in defense of rights. Rights, I shall argue, include second-order rights to protect their exercise with force if necessary. Second-order rights provide a basis on which the use of coercion by governmental institutions can be morally defended. But before turning to that issue, we need to examine a particular class of moral rights, the rights which are held by all persons simply as persons. For such rights hold the key to the moral assessment of coercion. Recognition of at least one central natural right, I will argue, makes clear why coercion requires a moral defense.

Notes

1. Ronald Dworkin, "The Original Position," *Chicago Law Review 40, no. 3 (Spring 1973): 500–533; reprinted in Norman Daniels, ed., Reading Rawls* (New York: Basic Books, 1976), 16–53, at pp. 38ff. Cf. Stanley I. Benn, "Rights," in Paul Edwards, ed., *The Encyclopedia of Philosophy* (New York: Macmillan and The Free Press, 1967), 7: 195–99.

2. A clear account of the differences between kinds of moral judgments and kinds of moral theories is given by William Frankena in his *Ethics*, 2d ed., (Englewood Cliffs, N.J.: Prentice-Hall, 1973), esp. chap. 1.

3. Jeremy Bentham, *An Introduction to the Principles of Morals and Legislation* (1789), ed. Laurence LaFleur (New York: Hafner Publishing Co., 1948), chaps. 1–5; John Stuart Mill, *Utilitarianism* (1861), ed. Samuel Gorovitz (Indianapolis: The Bobbs-Merrill Co., 1971), chaps. 1–2.

4. In Chapter 9, below, we will consider utilitarianism at some length in its specific application to punishment, and several of the issues involved in the discussion of utilitarian moral theory will arise once again.

5. Mill, *On Liberty* (1859), ed. Currin V. Shields (Indianapolis: The Bobbs-Merrill Co., 1956).

6. Mill attempts to provide and support a ranking of kinds of pleasure in *Utilitariansim*, but this has seemed to many a weak point of his argument. A nonutilitarian standard appears necessary to justify his ranking.

7. Wesley Hohfeld, *Fundamental Legal Conceptions* (New Haven: Yale University Press, 1923), p 38.

8. Hohfeld, *Fundamental Legal Conceptions*, p. 39.

9. Hohfeld, *Fundamental Legal Conceptions*, p. 51.

10. Hohfeld, *Fundamental Legal Conceptions*, p 60.

11. Benn, "Rights," *Encyclopedia of Philosophy*, 7: 195–99.

12. Stanley Benn and Richard S. Peters, *Social Principles and the Democratic State* (London: Allen and Unwin, Ltd., 1959), p 89: "Right and duty are names for the same normative relation, according to the point of view from which it is regarded." Cf. p. 98, where it is asserted that the existence of rights of animals is entailed by the existence of duties toward them.

13. Immanuel Kant, *The Doctrine of Virtue*, part 2 of *The Metaphysics of Morals*, ed. M. J. MacGregor (New York: Harper & Row, 1964), pp 98–103. Thomas E. Hill, Jr., has suggested some concrete examples of lack of fundamental self-respect which, he argues, support Kant's assertion of duties toward oneself; see his "Servility and Self-Respect," *The Monist* 57, no. 1 (January 1973): pp 87–104.

14. Examples given of liberties in the moral sense have included the right a person has to keep a dollar bill he finds in the street if he is the first to reach it, or the right each contestant has to win a race if he outdistances the other competitors. But these do not seem to be rights at all.

15. The second-order rights that, I shall argue below, are a part of moral rights do provide a parallel with legal claims, however.

16. For these reasons Benn in summarizing Hohfeld's categories refers to powers and immunities as "second-order rights," in a sense different from that proposed below; see "Rights," *Encyclopedia of Philosophy*, 7: pp 195–99.

17. H. L. A. Hart, "Are There Any Natural Rights?", *Philosophical Review* 64 (1955): pp 175–91; reprinted in Anthony Quinton, ed., *Political Philosophy* (Oxford: Oxford University Press, 1967),53–66. Hart's argument for the existence of an equal natural right of all to freedom is discussed in detail below.

18. Hobbes asserts that in a state of nature there is a "natural right of every man to every thing" which creates no corresponding moral duties in others, and he evidently intends to assert nothing stronger than a moral liberty or permission to act. A consequence of ruling out this sense of "right" is that Hobbes's right of nature is not a right at all. See *Leviathan* (1651), part. 1, chap. 14; ed. C. B. MacPherson (Baltimore: Penguin Books, 1968), p 189; ed. Michael Oakeshott (Oxford: Blackwell, 1960), p 84.

19. In some cases the duty is conditional on the conscious decision of the right-holder to engage in a particular activity. My duty not to impede another's voting makes requirements on me only when another person consciously undertakes to vote. But many rights are less specific in the activities they protect, and the exercise of these rights is correspondingly less tied to conscious decisions. The right to freedom of the person is a right to engage in whatever activities one chooses without interference; in this case the *exercise* of the right brings my duty to bear on my actions, but its exercise may not result from any conscious decision of the right-holder to exercise that particular right.

20. This sense of rights requires a formulation not entirely parallel with the others. The first clause of the other definitions has been omitted, since to say that X is at liberty not to suffer A seems to add nothing to Y's duty not to impose A on X. This class of rights, it might be noted, seems to be closest to Hohfeld's "immunities." A right$_2$ is not an immunity from certain kinds of action: one cannot say that an assault is not an assault simply because the victim has a right not to be assaulted, as one can say that a legal charge is not genuinely a legal charge because the accused has immunity from prosecution. But a right$_2$, unlike rights in the other senses, is a right not to be the subject of certain kinds of actions rather than a right to engage in specified activities.

21. Though there is surely an unconditional duty to contribute to the welfare of others, in appropriate circumstances, I am not sure that this is a duty based on a right. I am inclined to classify this as an irreducible moral duty rather than a duty created by a right. But whether welfare rights are rights$_3$ or rights$_4$ is inessential to my argument.

22. See, for example, Benn, "Rights"; Hart, "Natural Rights"; Joel Feinberg, "The Nature and Value of Rights," in *Rights, Justice, and the Bounds of Liberty* (Princeton: Princeton University Press, 1980), 143–58.

23. Hart, in "Natural Rights," 55–56, suggests that the concept of rights marks off a particular part of morality, the "morality of law," in which use of force is appropriate. I shall argue below, however, that force may be appropriate even in nonlegal contexts.

7
NATURAL RIGHTS

The purpose of the present study might be summarized by saying that we wish to know why coercion is usually wrong and when it is nevertheless right. In this chapter and the next I will provide answers to both questions which are built upon a theory of rights. The account I will offer of the moral presumption against coercion will be based on a defense of natural rights, or rather of one central natural right held by all persons. But the moral justification of coercion in certain circumstances also arises from certain aspects of the rights of persons, as I will argue in the next chapter.

It is a widely held assumption, in philosophical discussion as well as in a broader political context, that all persons have certain rights simply as persons. Everyone has the right that others keep their promises, for example, and a right to support from parents in childhood. Everyone has a right to choose her or his religious, political, and social affiliations freely, and a right not to be injured or assaulted. We all have certain natural or moral rights, in other words; these rights belong to all persons simply as persons and are not created by legal and social systems. Such rights are extrasocietal, not in the sense that they cannot be supported by the force of law or other social sanctions, but in the sense that they are rights which everyone has even in the absence of such support.

For the purposes of this discussion I shall accept this widely held assumption. We will assume that all persons do hold certain rights, simply as persons, and the moral status of coercion will be assessed with this initial assumption in mind. But the argument of the present chapter will also constitute a defense of that assumption, since I will try to show that treating others as persons in the moral sense requires us to recognize at least one fundamental natural right.

Several writers have put forward arguments for a central natural right to freedom and equality which begin by assuming that some of the specific rights enumerated above are universally held. I will begin exploration of the relationship between coercion and natural rights by considering some of these accounts. H. L. A. Hart, for example, has argued that recognition of any moral rights requires the assumption that all persons have a fundamental and equal right to freedom. His argument, useful as it is, seems to me weak at a crucial point. It will be discussed in the first portion of the present chapter, together with the attempts, which seem to me at least partially successful, of Gregory Vlastos and Richard Wasserstrom to fill in the omissions of Hart's argument. I shall argue instead that natural rights are grounded on considerations having to do with the nature of persons and of responsible action. The rights of persons may be understood as rights to act as responsible agents, and the conditions of responsibility show why it is that coercion infringes individuals' rights. This account will be developed further in the following chapter, where I offer the outline of a general theory of the structure and force of rights.

Hart's Defense of Natural Rights

A widely influential account of natural rights and their basis is that offered by H. L. A. Hart in his article, "Are There Any Natural Rights?"[1] The central argument of Hart's article is that recognition of any moral rights at all entails that there is at least one natural right, the right of all to be free.

His argument for this general right has two stages, corresponding to two kinds of moral right. A person may make a claim based on a right, Hart argues,

> (A) when the claimant has some special justification for interference with another's freedom which other persons do not have ("I have a right to be paid what you promised for my services"); (B) when the claimant is concerned to resist or object to some interference by another person as having no justification ("I have a right to say what I think").[2]

Rights created by promises, Hart says, are the clearest examples of special rights; freedom of speech and of religion are examples of general rights.

To assert a general right, Hart asserts, is to claim with respect to some specific class of actions the equal right of all to be free. General rights are specifications of the consequences of this natural right. But assertions of special rights, according to Hart, also presuppose this natural right. A right based on consent or on a promise counts as a right—as a justification for interfering with another's freedom—because the person who transferred the right has freely chosen to do so, in exercise of his equal right to be free. A right based on special status "is justified because it is fair; and it is fair because only so will there be an equal distribution of restrictions and so of freedom among this group of men."[3]

Therefore, both special and general moral rights presuppose that in the absence of certain special conditions which are consistent with the right being an equal right, any adult human being capable of choice has the right to forbearance on the part of all others from the use of coercion and restraint save to hinder coercion or restraint and is at liberty to do (i. e., is under no obligation to refrain from) any action which is not one coercing or restraining another or designed to injure other persons.[4] Hart sums up his argument thus:

> The assertion of general rights directly invokes the principle that all men equally have the right to be free; the assertion of a special right . . . invokes it indirectly.[5]

For clarity, we might represent the structure of Hart's argument as follows.

1. All moral rights are either general or special rights, in the sense specified above.
2. To claim a general right is to claim with respect to some particular action a fundamental right to freedom.
3. To claim a special right is to claim with respect to some particular action that others have acted in such a way as to permit an action which would otherwise violate their fundamental right to freedom.
4. The fundamental right whose existence is implied by the assertion of either a general or a special right is an equal right of all persons to freedom from coercion or restraint, except as it is necessary to prevent coercion or restraint.
5. Therefore, if there are any moral rights, there is a fundamental equal right of all to freedom.[6]

Hart's conclusion, he acknowledges, is conditional: *if* there are any moral rights, special or general, then there is at least this one natural right. A moral system which gives no recognition to rights at all, therefore, need not, so far as Hart's argument is concerned, recognize the basic right to be free. But anyone who grants that there are at least some moral rights is committed to this right.

It is not clear, however, that even this conditional conclusion can be validly drawn from Hart's premises. In the first place, why need every natural right be a right only to do actions which do not coerce or harm others? Moral rights are not commonly thought to be stronger than this. Few would argue that the right to an adequate living justifies theft. Yet in the absence of any reasons which exclude such a broad right, Hart's conclusion is not adequately supported by his argument.

According to Hobbes, the right of nature which is held by all in the absence of a sovereign power is "the Liberty each man hath, to use his own power, as he will himselfe, for the preservation of his own Nature, that is to say, of his own Life; and consequently, of doing any thing, which in his own Judgement, and Reason, hee shall conceive to be the aptest means thereunto." This right is subject to no restriction on whether the means adopted involve coercion or harm to others.[7] Needless to say, Hobbes's claim that there is such a natural right would find little support today. Nevertheless, what he is speaking of is quite properly called a right. An equal right more extensive than that proposed by Hart, therefore, appears to be consistent with the assertion of moral rights.

A more serious problem lies in the opposite direction. Need the recognition of moral rights commit one to a right as strong as Hart's, or even to any *equal* right at all? A special right, Hart says in the passage quoted above, imposes restrictions on the parties who stand in a special relationship to one another which are justified because they are fair, and fair because they bring about an equal distribution of restrictions and of freedom among all. But why need the distribution of freedom be equal? What prevents us from constructing a theory of rights, including natural rights, in which different persons are accorded fundamentally unequal rights?

It is not difficult to imagine such a theory. A doctrine of the divine right of kings, for example, might include the recognition of certain moral rights, such as the right of kings to rule, a right grounded in their special, divinely conferred status. It might also recognize the right of subjects to be treated fairly. The rights which such a theory asserts, surely, are moral rights. But they do not rest on an equal right of all to be free. Indeed, the rights just mentioned are grounded in a fundamental inequality between persons.

The doctrine of the divine right of kings, of course, has fallen from favor in contemporary political thought. Yet it illustrates the possibility of defending moral rights while rejecting the concept of equal rights. Consider also the rights which children have with respect to treatment by their parents. Children, surely, possess such rights, and yet the suggestion that their rights rest upon the equal right of all to be free is implausible. The *Declaration of the Rights of the Child* adopted by the United Nations in 1959, for example, follows its assertion of children's rights with an assertion of their need for "special protection" which is in "the best interests of the child." The child, it is asserted, has "the right to adequate nutrition, housing, recreation, and medical services," yet on the other hand "the child must not be admitted to employment before an appropriate minimum age."[8] Protections such as the last would clearly count as infringements of the rights of adults, and yet they are not for this reason unjust to children.

Clearly, on such a view the underlying rights to freedom of the two classes of persons are unequal. The *Declaration* argues in the same breath that children must not be deprived of their fundamental rights and that children must not be permitted to do certain things, regardless of their own decisions and desires, because such activities would be contrary to their interests. Paternalism, after all, is entirely appropriate as an element of the treatment of children. Indeed, to accuse someone of paternalism in his treatment of others is precisely to claim that he is treating others as if they were his children.

Hart might argue in reply that a system which rests on such a theory of rights is fundamentally unfair in that it distributes the natural right of freedom unequally. But why need all moral rights be based on fairness in Hart's sense? Hart's argument purports to show that there cannot be moral rights without an underlying equal right to freedom, but the examples that have been mentioned reveal that his argument is flawed.

Hart does not specifically mention the rights of children or incompetent adults.[9] The general right of all to be free is, he says, a right held equally by all adults capable of choice.[10] The rights of those who are not yet adults, or who due to mental incapacity or some other cause are not capable of choice, would presumably be less extensive. However, Hart's argument from special rights to an equal general right has the surprising consequence that children and mental incompetents either have the same general right to freedom as have normal adults or have no moral rights at all. For the recognition of any general or special moral right, according to Hart's account, must be grounded in a recognition of the equal right of all to be free. Persons who do not have the full measure of this right, therefore, cannot be ascribed any moral rights at all.

Hart's account of the nature and status of natural rights, therefore, is less than satisfactory. His argument from special and general rights to natural rights does not bear the weight which he places on it; moreover, its implications for natural rights of children and incompetents are quite unpalatable.

Other Defenses of Natural Rights

Among other writers who have offered arguments for an underlying natural right, two deserve mention because they strengthen Hart's

argument at its weakest point. Gregory Vlastos and Richard
Wasserstrom, in accounts influenced by Hart's treatment of natural
rights, have defended the presumption of equality of rights by linking
the moral status of rights with the intrinsic value of the activities or
objects which are the objects of claims based on rights.

Gregory Vlastos argues that every person, simply as a person, has a
right to equal well-being and equal freedom, where well-being refers
not to the quantity of goods owned by an individual but to the degree
to which his needs are satisfied. This natural right, he believes, is
fundamental to our conception of morality.[11] The basis for this right,
according to Vlastos, is that "the human worth of all persons is equal,
however unequal may be their merit."[12] Persons may be ranked by
their merit in any number of ways, but to do so is to grade individuals
in respect of their qualities, for "there is no way to grade individuals as
such."[13] To value an individual for his merit is not to value him as an
individual. Individuals, unlike animals and objects, are ends in themselves. Vlastos explicates this Kantian formula by saying that "everything other than a person can only have value *for* a person."[14]

Something may have value for a person in one of two ways: it may
be something which the person judges valuable in itself or it may be
the object of a person's choice. Human worth, accordingly, Vlastos
explains as the value of a person's enjoyment or well-being and the
value of his freedom to make choices. Human worth so understood
provides the basis for the right of all to equal well-being and freedom,
Vlastos argues in the following passage:

> Thus, to make a perfectly clear case, no matter how A and B might
> differ in taste and style of life, they would both crave relief from
> physical pain. In that case we would put the same value on giving
> this to either of them, regardless of the fact that A might be a
> talented, brilliantly successful person, B a "mere nobody." . . . In
> all cases where human beings are capable of enjoying the same
> goods, we feel that the intrinsic value of their enjoyment is the
> same. In just this sense we would hold that (1) *one man's well-being is
> as valuable as any other's.*

And a similar argument applies to the right to be free:

> We feel that choosing for oneself what one will do, believe, approve,
> say, see, read, worship, has its own intrinsic value, the same for all
> persons, and quite independently of the value of the things they
> happen to choose. . . . For us (2) *one man's freedom is as valuable as
> another's.*[15]

Therefore there underlies our system of morality a natural or human right—a right not dependent on special status, a right held by all persons against all others—to equal well-being and freedom.

Like Hart, Vlastos is here arguing from the ways in which we treat other persons—from the special and general rights we grant them, in Hart's case, or from our convictions about the value of persons and their activities, in Vlastos's version—to certain fundamental moral rights, stated in very general terms. Vlastos's argument is more explicit, however, in grounding fundamental rights in the notion of human worth. Moreover, his argument opens the possibility of legitimately unequal rights in a way that Hart's does not. If, on the one hand, children and mental incompetents have a value as persons equal to that of adults, Vlastos's argument implies that, unless there are compelling reasons to the contrary, they should have rights equal to those of adults. Yet it is possible to argue that less extensive rights for children are justified, at least in part, by their lesser capacity to enjoy the kinds of well-being and, especially, the kinds of freedom that are valued by adults. His argument for fundamental human rights does not require that these rights be equal if they exist at all.

Nevertheless, Vlastos's assertion that rights rest on equal value of enjoyment leads to problems of two kinds. First, it is difficult to know just what is meant by the assertion that "in all cases where human beings are capable of enjoying the same good, we feel that the intrinsic value of their enjoyment is the same."[16] If we take this claim in its most straightforward sense, its truth is questionable. Every person is capable of enjoying food; is every person's enjoyment of food therefore of equal value? Is a connoisseur's savoring a dish of Coquilles St. Jacques of intrinsic value equal to the eating of the same dish by a person of plain tastes who would have preferred a hamburger? Is the enjoyment of food by the starving of equal value to its enjoyment by the well-fed or the already overweight? It is difficult to know how to answer such questions, but Vlastos's account seems to require us to posit equal value in each case.

A second difficulty with the argument from equal enjoyment to equal rights lies in its suggestion that demonstrably unequal enjoyment be a sufficient basis for unequal rights. Does a person who is content with a loaf of bread and a jug of wine have a right only to that? What about a person who is desperately unhappy unless he is well supplied with sports cars, designer clothing, and pate with truffles? In such cases, should we abandon equality in distribution and strive instead for equal enjoyment?

Cases such as these are frequently invoked in arguments against utilitarian theories of justice, since the utilitarian appears to be committed to maximizing net satisfaction no matter how unequal the resulting distribution of goods. And—so the objection runs—justice is surely not served by pandering to the extravagant desires of a few. The objection I am raising here is not precisely the same. Vlastos never suggests that distribution of goods should be based on a calculation of the satisfaction of desires, and he speaks of well-being in general as having to do with the satisfaction of needs rather than desires. So perhaps the problem of "utility sinks" (or, in this case, "capacity for enjoyment sinks") can be dealt with by identifying the true needs of each individual and disregarding desires which have no basis in needs. And perhaps basic needs will prove, unlike desires, to be equal, or nearly so.

To deal with the troublesome cases in this way, however, would be a significant departure from Vlastos's general account. For he founds the right to well-being and freedom on universal subjective interests—on what we all in fact enjoy and want for ourselves—whereas an account based on needs would rely on objective interests which might not be supported by subjective preferences.[17]

Richard Wasserstrom tries to answer objections based on sharply unequal desires or needs by providing further support for Vlastos's argument at two points. In the first place, there are some goods, such as relief from physical pain, which all persons are equally capable of enjoying, or from which all persons are capable of deriving an equal enjoyment. If rights are based on the capacity for enjoyment, then in these cases equal capacity requires equal rights. Recognizing this fact provides a reason for equality of at least some rights. Second, in many areas, such as the ability to make choices, it is extremely difficult to say whether the capacities of persons are equal or unequal. Yet these areas have to do with basic human capacities and with activities and abilities which are central to a satisfying life. Since we recognize such areas of freedom as important to everyone, and since we have no clear criterion by which to determine whether individuals' capacities are equal or not, there is no better standard than equality for apportioning such freedoms. Wasserstrom thus offers a two-pronged argument for the right of all to equal well-being and equal freedom: in some cases all persons have equal capacities, while in other cases it is so difficult to decide whether this is the case or not, and yet so important to us to exercise these capacities, that the very difficulty of measuring capacity is an argument from uncertainty that the right should be equal.[18]

Wasserstrom's observations strengthen the case made by Vlastos for a fundamental natural right to well-being and freedom. For both, however, the equality of this right for all is based on the equality, known or presumed, of the capacity to enjoy it. The cases which seemed not to fit Hart's account are therefore still troublesome. What conclusions should we draw about rights in cases where individuals have obviously and substantially different capacities for enjoyment of certain freedoms, as in the case of parents and children? Do children's limited abilities diminish their rights?

If Hart's argument for a fundamental equal right of all to freedom could deal with such cases, the case against coercion might be grounded in such a right. The moral presumption against coercion might be built upon its infringement of this universal equal right. But neither Hart's account, nor the additional arguments of Vlastos and Wasserstrom, seem to me able to deal with such cases adequately. Rather than argue as Hart does from the existence of particular natural rights to a fundamental right to freedom, therefore, I shall instead develop the moral presumption against coercion on the basis of the connection between natural rights and the moral status of persons. Such an approach, I think, can accomplish the task which Hart attempts—identifying a central natural right which is the ground of other rights—while avoiding the difficulties we have found in Hart's insistence on equality.

Personhood and Responsibility

A fundamental premise which underlies all three of the accounts just discussed—Hart's, Vlastos's, and Wasserstrom's—is that every person ought to be *treated as a person*, or in other words that certain kinds of treatment are required and others proscribed on the basis of the moral standing that all persons possess. We can explicate the notion of moral personhood by linking it with the concept of *responsibility*, already discussed briefly above. To be treated as a person is to be treated as a moral agent, i.e., as one who is capable of responsible action. Persons are unlike animals and natural objects in that they are capable of making decisions and are responsible for their acts.

An agent is morally responsible for an act, it has been argued above, just in case two conditions obtain:

(i.) The agent knows what she is doing, i.e., knows what her act is and what are its likely consequences; and

(ii.) the act results from the agent's choice among the alternative actions open to her.[19]

Since responsibility is an essential element of personhood, to respect another as a person is to seek to preserve the conditions necessary for her to act responsibly.

It might appear that the argument just offered passes over the distinction between descriptive and normative statements in a way which is illogical or illegitimate. But such an impression is mistaken: the argument involves neither fallacy nor sleight of hand but rests rather on explication of the normative concept of personhood. To be a person is to be capable of acting responsibly. Given the normative premise that we are morally bound to respect persons as persons, it follows that we are required to behave toward them in ways which do not take away their ability to act responsibly, for to do so would be to treat them as something less than persons.

From this account of responsibility and its relation to personhood it follows that respect for the status of another as a person requires seeking to preserve the other's knowledge and freedom, the two conditions for her responsible action. We have found a simpler path, therefore, from personhood to the right of freedom than that suggested by Hart and Vlastos. Since acting responsibly is a necessary element of being a person, and since knowledge and freedom are necessary conditions of responsible action, the rights of all persons as persons include the right to freedom of choice among the alternative actions open to them.

The freedom which is necessary for responsibility is not merely freedom to bring one's actions into conformity with one's will. Rather, it goes beyond that limited sense of freedom to include freedom to make decisions and make them effective. It includes, in the terms employed earlier, not merely freedom to act but freedom to choose. Without freedom in this broader sense, genuine responsibility for one's actions may be absent.

The specific natural rights mentioned earlier can be seen as more concrete specifications of what it means to treat another as a person: to break one's promises to another casually, or to assault him, is to fail to give him the moral consideration he is due. An essential and central part of the respect due persons consists in recognizing and seeking to preserve the conditions for their responsible action. There is, therefore, a natural right of all persons, simply as persons, to freedom to choose, since such freedom is a condition necessary if they are to be able to act responsibly.

The Right to Self-Determination

Just as when we speak of freedom in general we implicitly invoke a range of normal activities and restraints from which we normally expect to be free, so the right to self-determination in general is a right to be free, within a range of normal activities, from an implied range of constraints on choice. We do not have a right to be rid of every obstacle to our freedom. There is no general right to freedom from our own inabilities and conflicting desires, for example. Although these may prevent us from making effective choices, we cannot expect to be rid of them by others' efforts.

Rather—just as when speaking of freedom in general we have in mind above all freedom from unwanted interference by others—the right to self-determination is above all a right to be free from others' interference with our making and carrying out choices. We expect of others that they will leave us free to order our lives as we will, and when that freedom is taken from us by others, the right to self-determination is infringed.

"Self-determination" is a more appropriate term than "autonomy" in describing this human right, although the terms are close in their meanings. Autonomy is a condition which needs to be achieved: a person may be free from external interference and yet act inconsistently, unthinkingly, or heedlessly. To be autonomous means to set one's own laws and standards and to follow them, and a person such as I have described has not achieved autonomy. Nevertheless he is able to determine his future condition by his choices, and he does enjoy self-determination. The latter is more immediately the concern of political institutions, the former of individual moral development.

Self-determination requires more than freedom to *act:* it also requires freedom to *choose,* in the sense described earlier.[20] A person has a right not only to do the action he prefers, given the circumstances, but also to have a choice among alternatives which are not constricted by another's acts. But self-determination does not require *independence* of others. A person who voluntarily submits to another's authority has not surrendered his control over his future but has chosen to exercise it in a way which limits his freedom to make certain subsequent choices. To submit voluntarily to monastic authority, or to enter into a contract which allows another to require certain future actions, is not to violate but to exercise the right to self-determination.[21]

The basis of the fundamental right to self-determination, like that of other natural rights, must be sought in an understanding of what it means to treat someone as a person. To be a person is to have moral standing, to be capable of moral choice and responsible for one's actions. To treat someone as a person is to treat her in ways which are consistent with that moral standing and to recognize that for the other person, as for oneself, the making and carrying out of choices is of central importance. Persons make decisions, act, and shape their futures by their actions: that is what it means to be a person, and that is what distinguishes persons from mere objects or organisms.

There is a conceptual tie, therefore, between personhood and basic human rights. Unless we recognize the importance of another's making and carrying out her own choices—choices of where to live, what to say, what to believe, and the like—we do not recognize her as a person, and if we act in ways which prevent her from exercising her capacity to choose, we violate her rights as a person. Recognition of the right of self-determination is part of what it means to treat others as persons.

This account of the basis of the right of self-determination is by no means complete. I have not offered any reasons, for example, why we *ought* to treat others as persons. Rather, I am relying on the assumption that this is a basic element of acting morally. Nor have I offered reasons why treating others as persons must lead to equal rights for all. Indeed, it is an advantage of the account I have offered of the basis of natural rights that it does not rule out the possibility that some natural rights, such as those of children and parents, may be unequal.

At the same time, there is a strong presumption in favor of equality of basic human rights, and it is surely only in special cases, such as that of children, that we are willing to countenance inequalities in natural rights. The presumption of equality can also be grounded, I believe, in the concept of moral personhood: we are all equally persons, after all, whatever inequalities of ability or achievement may exist among us. But the moral presumption against coercion which I offer, based on the right to self-determination, does not rest essentially on the equality of natural rights but only on the possession of this right by all persons. Whatever we say about the difficult cases for equality of rights, therefore, the resolution of these cases is not essential for the account of coercion which will be offered in the next chapter.

Alienability and Absoluteness

Before turning to the status of coercion in the context of the right to self-determination, we should take brief note of two further properties which natural rights are claimed to have. According to the traditional doctrine of natural rights, such rights are both absolute and inalienable.[22] Does the right to self-determination have these features?

Let us consider first the question of alienability. Some rights may be transferred from one person to another by contract, agreement, or another voluntary act. Property rights may be transferred to a buyer by selling a piece of property, for example, or given up to an unknown future user by abandonment. To give up the basic right to self-

determination would require an agreement to subject oneself completely and irrevocably to the direction of another—a contract to
become the slave of another person, for example, agreeing to become
another's property to use as he chooses.

Such an agreement would be possible, to be sure; but it would be
morally wrong. To transfer one's basic human right would in effect be
to deny one's standing as a moral person. A slave is not responsible for
the acts he commits at the direction of his owner, and to the extent that
he has lost the responsibility for his own acts he has ceased to act as a
person or to be treated by others—by his owner, first of all, but also by
others who recognize that his acts are not his own—as a person.

It is the denial of personhood that makes forced slavery such a
grievous wrong. Even voluntary slavery is objectionable, on similar
grounds: a person ought not to give up his standing as a person even
by his own choice. To do so would be to violate a duty toward himself
and to abdicate his duty to the moral community to play a part in it.[23]
We ought not to allow a person to give up his right to self-determination voluntarily.

The reasons for prohibiting the transfer of the right to self-determination, it may be noted, are moral reasons which are not simply
consequences of the existence of that right. The idea of slavery is
morally repugnant, but it is not illogical; nor is it inconsistent to hold
that most people have a right to self-determination but that slaves have
no such right. So our conclusion that this right is—as the natural
rights tradition suggests—an *inalienable* right is grounded in normative
considerations, not simply in the nature of rights or of this right. The
reasons for this judgment are moral rather than conceptual.

The question of whether the right to autonomy is *absolute* has been
the subject of a good deal of debate. Some defenders of natural rights
have denied that they are absolute, on the grounds that there are
circumstances in which any of the traditional natural rights must be
overridden. Frankena and Brandt have suggested that natural rights
are "prima facie rights,"[24] rights which are analogous to prima facie
claims at law.[25] Their account of rights is parallel to W. D. Ross's
argument that duties may be divided into duties all things considered
and prima facie duties.[26] The right of free speech may not be exercised
in such a way as to constitute a danger to others' safety, Brandt argues,
as by shouting "Fire!" in a crowded theater. And "substantially the
same thing can be said about any other specific right one can mention:
We can conceive of times when such rights must give way, and,
therefore, they are only prima facie and not absolute rights."[27]

Brandt's premises are sound, but his conclusion does not follow
from them. The distinction which Ross suggests between prima facie

duties and duties per se is useful because, in cases where one duty is outweighed by another, the first duty ceases to bind us in any way. It is this feature of the concept of duty which makes the distinction appropriate. When keeping one's promise to meet a friend would require failing to rescue a drowning man, one does not have a duty to keep this particular promise. A prima facie duty which is overridden by a stronger or more urgent duty is no longer a duty at all. *Duty*—or *moral duty* at any rate—is a term which connotes a final moral evaluation. Although a person might say, "I have a duty to do X, but I prefer to do Y," it does not make sense to say "I have a duty to do X but I ought to do Y." The latter could sensibly be asserted only in exceptional circumstances—if one intended by the assertion to deny that duty is the fundamental moral category (if a utilitarian uttered it, for example, using "duty" ironically to mean "what I am required to do by your misguided deontological ethics") or intended to contrast the duty attached to a certain institutional role with moral obligation ("I have a duty as an officer of the law to arrest this man, but under the circumstances I think I really ought to let him go").

But rights are unlike duties in these respects. When the rights of two persons come into conflict neither of them ceases to be a right in the way in which one of two conflicting duties ceases to be a duty. The fact that rights are sometimes overridden by other rights or by other moral considerations does not show that the rights in question are prima facie or less than absolute rights. In any social organization each individual's freedom of choice is limited in order to protect the safety and freedom of others. But the necessity, and the moral permissibility, of such limits does not make the rights which are thereby infringed something less than rights.

The right to self-determination is an absolute right in that it is always a ground for a claim that it be respected. The right always constitutes a reason why it should not be violated. It is not an absolute right in the sense that it can never justly be violated; in this very strong sense, no rights are absolute. But it is an absolute right in that even when it may or must be violated its status as a right remains, and its violation is a moral cost. To deny that the right is a right in such circumstances is to fail to perceive the distinctive moral character of rights.

Herbert Morris has put a similar point forcefully:

It is seriously misleading to turn all justifiable infringements into noninfringements by saying that the right is only prima facie, as if we have, in concluding that we should not accord a man his rights, made out a case that he had none. To use the language of "prima facie rights" misleads, for it suggests that a presumption in favor of the existence of a right has been overcome in these cases where all that can be said is that the presumption in favor of according a man his right can be overcome. If we begin to think the right itself is prima facie, we shall in cases in which we are justified in not according it, fail sufficiently to bring out that we have interfered where justice says we should not. Our moral framework is unnecessarily and undesirably impoverished by the theory that there are such rights.[28]

The right of all to self-determination, then, is a natural right in the traditional sense: it is a right held by all persons simply as persons and not as a result of any particular acts, theirs or others', or of any special relationship. It is an inalienable right; and it is an absolute right, in the sense that it always constitutes a reason for noninterference.[29]

Notes

1. H. L. A. Hart, "Are There Any Natural Rights?", *Philosophical Review* 64 (1955): 175–91; reprinted in Anthony Quinton, ed., *Political Philosophy* (Oxford: Oxford University Press, 1967), 53–66.
2. Hart, "Natural Rights," 60. Special rights and general rights, it may be noted, correspond closely to *jura in personam* and *jura in rem* in law. Cf. Wesley Hohfeld, *Fundamental Legal Conceptions* (New Haven: Yale University Press, 1923), chap. 2.
3. Hart, "Natural Rights," 66.
4. Hart, "Natural Rights," 53.
5. Hart, "Natural Rights," 64.
6. See Hart, "Natural Rights," 64: this is almost precisely Hart's own summary, immediately preceding the passage just quoted.
7. Thomas Hobbes, *Leviathan* (1651), part. 1, chap. 14; ed. C. B. MacPherson (Baltimore: Penguin Books, 1968), 189; ed. Michael Oakeshott (Oxford: Blackwell, 1960), 84. (I follow MacPherson rather than Oakeshott in retaining Hobbes's spelling and punctuation.) Hobbes held that apart from a state the notions of right and wrong have no application, but his description of the right of nature can be taken as an assertion of a right even apart from the state.
8. *United Nations Declaration of the Rights of the Child*, reprinted in Onora O'Neill and William Ruddick, eds., *Having Children* (New York: Oxford University Press, 1979), 112–14; the passages quoted are from Principles 2, 5, and 9.
9. Hart mentions a "parent's moral right to obedience from his child" as an example of a special right arising from a personal relationship, but he does not recognize that this example leads to serious problems with his general account; see "Natural Rights," 63.
10. Hart, "Natural Rights," 53.
11. Gregory Vlastos, "Justice and Equality," in A. I. Melden, ed., *Human Rights* (Belmont, Calif.: Wadsworth Publishing Co., 1970), 76–95. This article constitutes the first two parts of the article published under the same title in Richard Brandt, ed., *Social Justice* (Englewood Cliffs, N.J.: Prentice-Hall, Inc., 1962).
12. Vlastos, "Justice and Equality," 86.
13. Vlastos, "Justice and Equality," 87.
14. Vlastos, "Justice and Equality," 91.
15. Vlastos, "Justice and Equality," 93–94.
16. Vlastos, "Justice and Equality," 93.

17. On the essential differences between these two kinds of standards, see T. M. Scanlon, "Preference and Urgency," *Journal of Philosophy* 72, no. 19 (6 November 1975): 655–69.

18. Richard Wasserstrom, "Rights, Human Rights, and Racial Discrimination," in Melden, ed., *Human Rights*, 106–7.

19. See chap. 3, above.

20. See chap. 4, above, and further discussion of this distinction in chap. 8, below.

21. A similar right—the right of all persons "to conduct their own affairs in pursuit of their own interests"—is defended as the foundation of all rights by A. I. Melden in *Rights and Persons* (Berkeley: University of California Press, 1977), esp. chaps. II and VI.

22. See, for example, Benn and Peters, *Social Principles*, 96; absoluteness is taken as a distinctive feature of the natural rights doctrine, and one which shows the whole doctrine to be mistaken, in J. D. Mabbott, *The State and the Citizen* (London: Arrow, 1958), 57–58; cited in Wasserstrom, "Rights, Natural Rights, and Racial Discrimination," 97. Vlastos observes that the absoluteness of natural rights is not explicitly asserted by Locke and questions whether it is reasonably inferred from his account; see "Justice and Equality," 81.

23. I am assuming that the contract to enter into voluntary slavery is made freely and with full knowledge of what one is doing. It might be argued that this is impossible—that one cannot know in advance what a contract to give up one's right to self-determination means. If that is the case, then there is no such thing as truly voluntary slavery, and the objections mentioned above do not even come into play.

24. William Frankena, symposium paper on "The Concept of Universal Human Rights," in American Philosophical Association, *Science, Language, and Human Rights* (Philadelphia: University of Pennsylvania Press, 1952), 189–207; Richard B. Brandt, *Ethical Theory* (Englewood Cliffs, N.J.: Prentice-Hall, 1959), chap. 17, "Human Rights."

25. On prima facie claims in law and morals see Feinberg, "Nature and Value of Rights."

26. W. D. Ross, *The Right and the Good* (Oxford: The Clarendon Press, 1930), chap. 2.

27. Brandt, *Ethical Theory*, 446.

28. Herbert Morris, "Persons and Punishment," *Monist* 52, no. 4 (October 1968): 475–501; in Melden, ed., *Human Rights*, 111–35, at 132–33. In one respect Morris is imprecise: it is not necessary that justice be overruled by some other moral consideration. Justice itself may require that one person's rights yield to another's.

29. I have not mentioned above a third traditional property of natural rights: their imprescriptibility. Clearly, this attribute also holds of the right to self-determination—surely no one could acquire rights to limit a person's basic freedom of choice, rights which he previously lacked, simply by interfering with him regularly over a period of time. I relegate this property to a footnote because its denial is so implausible. Some of the traditional natural rights lack this property under existing laws, however, e. g., the right to exclusive use and possession of property. In most American jurisdictions the right to use of property, and in some cases actual title to property, may be acquired by its regular use, provided either that its use is necessary as a means of access to property owned by the user or that the owner of the property used makes no attempt to discourage or prevent its use. But property rights, of course, are also alienable. If there is an inalienable and imprescriptible right to property, it must be a general right to use and acquire property, not a particular right to any item of property. On prescriptibility see Vlastos, "Justice and Equality," 82–83 and n. 25; "Prescriptive Rights and Easement to Title," *Dictionary of Business Law*, in Clarence L. Barnhart, ed., *American College Encyclopedic Dictionary* (Chicago: Spencer Press, 1952), Encyclopedic Supplements, 291–92.

8
COERCION AND THE STRUCTURE
OF RIGHTS

In the previous chapter it has been argued that the moral status of persons is the basis for natural rights and that a central element in treating others as persons is recognition of their fundamental right to self-determination. This right is the right to make one's own choices and to make them effective in shaping one's future actions and circumstances.

The present chapter will set out the moral status of coercion in the context of this universal right. In doing so, it will be necessary to examine more closely exactly what it is that we assert when we assert that a person has a right of one kind or another. Our examination of the moral status of coercion, therefore, will lead us to an analysis of the distinct components of rights, especially of what we will call "first-order" and "second-order" rights, which will help to identify both the wrongness of coercion in most circumstances and the reasons which justify it in some circumstances. A theory of the nature and content of rights, therefore, will prove helpful in explicating both the immorality and the moral justification of coercion.

Coercion and the Right to Self-Determination

The right to make one's own choices and make them effective is limited by many different kinds of acts and conditions. One of the most effective is intentional and forceful interference by others. Such interference may take the form of deliberate injury, physical compulsion, threat, or the like. It is above all against these limits on self-determination that persons have a right, based upon their moral status as persons, to be free.

The victim of a coercive threat remains able to act freely, since he chooses between the alternatives of complying with the coercer's demand and defying the threat. Nevertheless his ability to determine his future condition by his actions is severely restricted. There are choices for him to make, but the nature of these choices has been altered in important respects by the coercer. The coercer has not taken from her victim the ability to act on the basis of choice, as she would have if she had subjected him to physical compulsion instead. But she has taken from him the ability to make his choices effective in shaping the future course of his life according to his will and desires, and she has done so by interposing a threat motivated by her own desires.

The victim's choice still determines his future condition: if he complies with the threat he will be spared the threatened penalty (provided the threat is genuinely conditional), and if he does not he will suffer the penalty, unless he overpowers or escapes the threatener. But the range of probable outcomes has been resticted by the coercer's actions and declared intentions. The victim cannot choose to act in such a way as to bring about the future condition he desires in the usual way, for the threat has drastically changed the expected outcome of his actions.

Everything that has been said so far applies to noncoercive as well as coercive threats. What distinguishes coercion is that the penalty threatened is not one which the victim can reasonably tolerate as a cost of defying the threat. The victim has no choice but to comply, in the sense that the penalty is sufficient to make it unreasonable to submit to it rather than perform the act demanded. In comparison with noncoercive duress, coercion imposes no further restriction on the victim's *freedom to act*, in the sense discussed above, since it is still physically possible for the victim to defy the threat. But it is an even more severe infringement on *freedom to choose*, since there is only one course of action available to the agent which has expected consequences that he can reasonably choose to bring upon himself.

The reason why coercion is wrong, therefore, is that it infringes the victim's freedom to choose how he will act and to shape his future condition by his choices. The case against coercion is based on the victim's right to self-determination. Coercion interferes with the victim's exercise of this right. It is a violation of the victim's right and a violation of the coercer's duty to respect this natural right.

Two aspects of the relation between coercion and the right to self-determination should be noted. First, it is essential to the moral case against coercion that the coercer declare to the victim her intention of harming him if he does not comply. Second, it is also essential that a threat of harm and not an offer of reward be involved.

To take up the second matter first: A coercer forces her victim to act in a certain way by attaching the cost of intolerable harm to any other course of action. The victim has no choice but to comply. If she instead offers a reward for the desired behavior, she does not commit the same kind of direct violation of the other's right to freedom of choice. Attaching an undesirable consequence to a particular action makes that action less eligible for the agent's choice, and a coercive threat makes the action to which it is attached effectively ineligible, since it would not be reasonable to choose it with the attached penalty. Coercion narrows the range of available outcomes among which a person may reasonably choose to just one and thus destroys freedom of choice.

An offer is not normally sufficient to render every alternative action effectively unavailable. It alters the situation of the person to whom it is made, making one action together with its expected outcome more desirable than it would otherwise have been. But it does not reduce the number of alternatives available or take away the person's ability to choose effectively among them. In special circumstances, however— those in which offers in effect constitute threats—the good offered may be something that the person to whom the offer is made needs so urgently that he cannot but choose to accept the offer. An offer made under such circumstances—an offer to save a drowning man if he does some act, for example—*is* a violation of the right to self-determination, and the moral case against such offers is the same as that against coercion. The conditional offer of the necessary means of avoiding intolerable harm constitutes coercion.[1]

To return to the first point mentioned: The coercer must declare her intention of harming the victim if he does not comply. The intention to inflict harm does not infringe the right to self-determination, nor can it coerce, unless the victim knows of the intention. The intent need not be communicated verbally: a pistol aimed in my direction and an outstretched hand communicate with indisputable clarity a coercive threat. But some means of communicating the intent is essential.

Coercion and Other Restrictions on Freedom

In the account of coercion that has been offered in chapters 2 and 3, above, the focus was on the effect of coercion on the victim, and it was therefore essential to distinguish coercion from less severe threats that are insufficient to coerce. From the victim's point of view the distinction between coercion and duress is an extremely important one, since it delimits those actions for which the agent is not liable to blame. In considering coercion as a means of influencing behavior, however, we are looking at the concept from the point of view of the person making the threat. And from this perspective the line between coercion and duress is less important—indeed, it is impossible to draw precisely, since a necessary condition for a threat to be coercive is that it be effective, and it is the victim's act, not the threatener's, which makes it effective. The distinction between coercion and duress from the threatener's point of view is much more a matter of degree, shading from mild threats which are virtually certain not to coerce to severe threats which are sufficient to coerce any normal person.

For that reason we cannot really ask whether a person is justified in employing coercion to influence behavior. For whether a threat is coercive is not wholly determined by the threat itself. Rather, the moral question we must ask is whether a person is justified in *attempting* to coerce another. And this amounts to several questions: is it permissible to make threats, to try to influence others' acts by threats, and in particular to attempt influence by severe threats which may be expected to compel the victim's choice? The question of whether coercion is morally worse than duress simply cannot be answered, for this distinction cannot be drawn from the point of view of the threatener. We must ask instead whether certain kinds and degrees of threats are justifiable means of influence.

The wrongness of threats is more or less proportional to the wrongness of the harm threatened. It is worse to break someone's arm than to slap him; so the threat of the former is proportionally more serious, and hence more wrong, than the threat of the latter. So much seems evident.

It might seem equally obvious that actually inflicting a harm is always worse than merely threatening it. But in fact this need not be so. The threat of a slap on the wrist may be worse, because of the apprehension it causes, than the slap itself. But to attempt to *coerce* by means of a threat is worse than simply making a threat, since coercion involves not only a threat to inflict harm but also an attempt to control the victim's actions.

With these differences between harms and threats in mind, we might ask: are there harms which cannot justifiably be imposed but may nevertheless be threatened? May a person, or a state, threaten harms which it could not morally inflict in order to influence the behavior of individuals or of other states?

The justifiability of bluffing is a crucial assumption of the doctrine of military deterrence in foreign policy: in order to ensure peace in the world, it is claimed, the United States must convince the other nations of the world that it is ready to employ nuclear weapons as a last resort against enemy aggression, even if it would be morally wrong ever to carry out this threat. Several theoretical discussions of the so-called paradoxes of deterrence have supported the view that it is sometimes morally permissible to threaten what it would be immoral to do.[2] It is possible to defend a policy of deterrence which does not rest on bluffing only if one is willing to countenance the actual use of nuclear weapons in warfare, either in a first strike intended to overwhelm conventional forces and bring an enemy to its knees or in retaliation for an enemy's first strike. Traditional doctrines of morality in warfare, including the set of principles which arise from the "just war doctrine" in Christian ethics, categorically condemn the use of weapons of such extensive and indiscriminate destructive power. The only available justification for the possession of nuclear weapons, therefore, is as a means of bluffing. A nation which holds nuclear weapons solely for the purpose of threatening, with no intention of using them, will of course not publish this fact openly, since to do so would undermine the credibility of its bluff. But even a public declaration that nuclear weapons will not be used would not completely undermine the perceived threat of their use, since an enemy could never be certain of the sincerity of the declaration, and the remaining uncertainty would probably still be sufficient to deter others from launching an attack. The argument is frequently made, therefore, that nuclear deterrence is an example of the justified threat of a penalty which it would be wrong to carry out.

For several reasons I find the argument just sketched in support of nuclear deterrence seriously inadequate. Whatever judgment one may draw about the effectiveness of the nuclear deterrent threat in preventing attack and preserving stability, to show such a threat to be morally justified it is necessary to show not only that it has a beneficial effect but also that it is morally preferable to any alternative means of achieving the same end. Moreover, the scale of harm which is at stake in the threat to employ nuclear weapons is so vast that analogies with more familiar kinds of threats break down: a threat which places the entire human world at risk strains our capacities for moral assessment and colors our perception of all else. To explore these issues with the care they demand would divert us from the topics at hand.[3] All the same, such examples are obviously relevant case studies in the justifiability of the threats, and even if the nuclear deterrent threat itself rests on a questionable moral basis, it seems likely that there are at least some justifiable threats of unjustifiable harm. We must consider the possibility that the morality of actions and the morality of threats might thus diverge.

Since the difference between coercion and other means of influencing behavior is not entirely controlled by the coercer, justification is inescapably a matter of degree. The more serious the harm threatened, the greater the wrong done to the person threatened. A threat of any kind is an intrusion into another's affairs. A conditional threat always carries with it, in addition to the undesirability of a threat of any kind, an attempt to control another's actions. This additional element directly contravenes the victim's ability to choose his actions and his future circumstances freely. For this reason, any attempt to control through threats undermines the victim's right to self-determination. We cannot draw any categorical conclusions about the justifiability of coercive as opposed to noncoercive threats, for the reasons already mentioned: in discussing the justifiability of a threat we are considering the blame which the coercer deserves, but coercive threats cannot be distinguished from other threats until the victim responds. In general, however, it is clear that coercive threats are more serious, and therefore more morally objectionable, than threats insufficient to coerce.

Threats are not the only impediment to the right to self-determination. Many other events and circumstances, not all of human doing, may have the effect of hindering a person's freedom to choose. A hiker is barred from taking a certain trail if he sees an impassable tangle of fallen trees—barred just as effectively as by a gunman who threatens to shoot him if he proceeds. If is not just human interference but physical limits, natural dangers, and a host of other obstacles that diminish our ability to choose freely.

Why, then, should we attach so much importance to removing the humanly-created limits on freedom? The answer has to do with the treatment that we expect to be given by others and with what we want from a system of social rules and institutions. Human interference is within the power of other persons to avoid, and it is within the power of social institutions to affect, e. g., by making and enforcing laws. We expect others to leave us free to carry on our lives without the interposition of injury or threat. Furthermore, we want a social system to secure this freedom, insofar as possible, for all persons. Natural limits on self-determination are not so readily subject to social control.

Nonhuman hindrances to freedom are also aspects of our lives that we accept as more or less unavoidable. We adapt to them and are willing to live with them; they are not among the obstacles to freedom that we expect to be freed from. Knowing that physical obstacles and limits do not depend on others' decisions and acts, we do not claim freedom from these restraints and dangers as our right. But freedom from coercion—since coercion results from others' voluntary acts in disregard for our rights—is a condition which we desire and which we expect social institutions to secure.

To be sure, natural impediments to freedom can also be removed or diminished by concerted social action. To the extent that this is possible, freedom from such restraints may be something which we expect social institutions to provide for us. This is particularly true of obstacles whose removal requires social cooperation on a large scale. We do not expect our governments to clear the fallen branches out of our driveways; that is something we are able and willing to do for ourselves. We do expect governmental agencies to remove major and unexpected obstacles—to provide the necessary equipment, or at least to coordinate efforts, to clear a landslide from a major highway, for example. But if any rights are involved here, they are rights held with respect to social institutions. We have no rights with respect to trees and landslides, since they are not capable of having corresponding duties toward us. Moreover, physical obstacles do not carry with them the element of personal affront, of disregard for one's moral status, that is part of the wrong done by coercion. Building roads through mountains and bridges over rivers, building dams to control floods, and providing either training or machines to overcome inabilities are all ways of extending individuals' freedom from nonhuman obstacles. But the obstacles that are removed by these means are not infringements of our rights.

All of these obstacles can be counted as impediments to freedom: each effectively blocks us from doing certain things that we might want to do. But we do not have a right to the greatest possible degree of freedom. Rather, we have a right to be free of unreasonable and unexpected interference with our freedom to act and to choose. Others' threats and forceful interference are the most direct infringements of the freedom to which we have a right.

To the extent that nonhuman obstacles are limits on our freedom to make effective choices and are removable by social institutions, we may expect or demand their removal. But the obstacles themselves are not violations of our rights. Our right to self-determination is denied, above all, by coercion and other forms of human interference, and it is the removal of such obstacles to freedom that we may demand as a matter of right.

Force and Second-Order Rights

In the previous chapter I proposed a definition of rights. A person has a right, I suggested, just in case he is at liberty with respect to an action or a thing and others have a duty either not to interfere, not to refuse to assist, or to assist the right-holder in doing or having what is his by right.[4] We need now to consider the consequences of having a right in circumstances in which the right is violated or appears likely to be violated. For it is in such circumstances that the use of force in defense of one's rights may be justified. In this concluding section of the present chapter I shall explore the appropriateness of force by further analyzing the nature and structure of rights. On this basis I shall offer a standard for determining whether and when coercion is justified which is broad in its range of application.

An example may make clearer the connection of force with rights. Suppose that a person has property rights to a certain piece of land. What is the moral force of this assertion of right? First, the right affords the owner of the liberty to use the land as he will. Second, those with respect to whom he has this right—all others, presumably, or all others in a certain community—have a duty not to interfere with his use of the land and to use it themselves only in ways which the owner permits. These consequences follow from the definition of rights offered in chapter 6, above. The two elements mentioned are entailed by a right$_1$, in the sense defined there; stronger forms of rights include additional claims on others beyond mere noninterference.

Now suppose that another person indicates that she intends to take the land from its owner or to use it in ways that the owner has not approved. An additional element is included in the property right of the owner: he is also justified in undertaking to prevent the other person from interfering with his exclusive use and control over his land.

There are a number of ways in which the owner might do this. He might tell the other person, "Please don't do that." Or he might kill her. The former is justified, but likely ineffective, while the latter, though effective, is unjustified. Property rights do not license the owner to prevent their infringement by any means whatever.

The consequences of having a right become clearer if we compare a case where no breach of rights in involved with a situation in which a right is at stake. Suppose that Stan has declared that he intends to commit a breach of duty toward Laurel. He intends to do something extremely unkind, for example. Though his act will displease and possibly harm Laurel, it will not violate Laurel's rights. In such a case it is permissible for Laurel to try to prevent Stan from carrying out his intention in several ways. He may admonish him, try to persuade him, plead with him. But he may not *force* him not to do as he intends. It is not permissible for him to physically restrain or to threaten Stan.

But if Stan's intention is to violate Laurel's rights, Laurel is justified not only in attempting to persuade but also, if necessary, in forcing him to refrain. If in this case Laurel physically restrains Stan or induces him to refrain from the intended action by a coercive threat, he may defend his act by citing his right that the action not be done to him.

These observations, I believe, are further elaborations of what we mean when we assert that someone has a right. When we recognize that a person has a right to exclusive use of a piece of property, we recognize implicitly that he may use force or coercion if necessary to protect that right. Among the ways in which he may do this are posting "Keep Off" signs, thereby attempting to keep trespassers away by admonition; putting up fences, thereby (if the fences are sufficiently high and strong) exercising a kind of physical compulsion; or posting signs and publishing notices threatening harm to those who use his land without permission.

The appropriateness of force or coercion in relation to rights to vigorously defended by Kant in his analysis of the concept of justice. What sets justice apart from other moral concepts, Kant argues, is just this feature: obligations of justice which another has toward me are obligations which I may compel her to fulfill.[5] Thus, according to Kant:

> When it is said that a creditor has a right to demand from his debtor the payment of a debt, this does not mean that he can persuade the debtor that his own reason itself obligates him to this performance; on the contrary, to say that he has such a right means only that the use of coercion to make anyone do this is entirely compatible with everyone's freedom, including the freedom of the debtor, in accordance with universal laws. Thus "right" and "authorization to use coercion" mean the same thing.[6]

To have a right is to have the moral authority or permission—i.e., to have the right—to prevent violation of one's right. I shall refer to the right to prevent violations of one's rights as a *second-order right*. And this right can be seen to be included implicitly in every right, whether a right$_1$, a right$_2$, a right$_3$, or a right$_4$, using the categories offered in chapter 6. Every right, in other words, includes a second-order right.[7] This thesis draws its support from the way in which rights enter into the moral evaluation of actions. Force and coercion are prima facie wrong, because they take from their victims the freedom to choose their actions in the usual way. The assertion of the need to protect a right, however, is a defense for the use of force and coercion. The moral basis of this defense is the second-order right each person has to protect the exercise of his rights.

Every right, moral or legal, includes a second-order right to protect or secure its exercise; but not every right includes the right to use force. Rather, the second-order right is a right to use necessary and appropriate means. If a person promises me that she will help me fix my car, I have a moral right that she carry out her promise. If she fails to offer her help when I need it, I have a second-order right to obtain the help she promised. I may reproach her with her failure to live up to her promise, and I may remind her that she has a duty to do so. Perhaps I may even threaten to tell her friends that she does not live up to her promises, if she fails to respond to my urging. There are several things I may do, in other words, that I would not be justified in doing if she had merely offered to help me sometime or had made neither a promise nor an offer. But I may not use force, or threaten dire consequences, to get her to carry out her promise.

The second-order right is a right to use whatever means are necessary and appropriate to secure or protect the exercise of the right. Clearly, the means which are appropriate must be judged according to the urgency or importance of the right which is in question. The moral right that another person keep her promise to fix my car is insufficient to justify use of force; the moral right to basic freedom of the person is of sufficient importance to do so. To specify exactly what rights can justify forceful means in their defense would be difficult, and any proposal is likely to be subject to dispute. Yet at least one generalization can be offered; all rights which are basic human rights—those which express the fundamental right to self-determination and which are thus implied by our moral standing as persons— carry with them a second-order right to employ force if necessary.

When a person uses force to protect her rights, she may defend her action on the ground that it was necessary to prevent a violation of right. In saying so she is asserting her own assessment of the circumstances. Another person, she might explain, had threatened to interfere with her enjoyment of her rights, or had behaved in a way which implied that he would do so and had not been dissuaded by admonitions.

But of course the claim that force is necessary may be mistaken. The situation is similar to that posed by a claim of right: a right is a moral defense for acting in a certain way, but a person's claim that her action was justified as an exercise of her rights may be wrong. In such a case, even if the person has the right she claims, the right does not justify the action. The same holds for a misjudgment that force is necessary to defend a right. A person who beats up an innocent passerby, claiming that doing so was necessary to prevent him from stealing his watch, cannot justify his act by his second-order right to his property, any more than a person can morally defend roasting his neighbor's child on a spit by invoking the right to practice his Molochian religion.

There is a peculiar appropriateness about the use of *coercion* to protect rights, however, since coercion, when it is successful, involves no actual use of force but only the threat of its use. When a person induces another to refrain from violating his basic rights by a coercive threat, he does not actually use force or violence against the potential attacker. If the other person defies the threat and acts in disregard for his rights nonetheless, the right-holder may legitimately prevent him forcibly from doing so, nonforceful means having been proven ineffective. To deter the other by a coercive threat does deprive him of a measure of freedom to make and carry out choices. But the interference posed by coercion is less serious and less objectionable, in such circumstances, than that posed by actual physical force.

Among the elements of the concept of rights, therefore, we must count not only correlative duties of others but also second-order rights to protect the exercise of rights with appropriate means, including forceful means when necessary and appropriate. If everyone has a right to an adequate diet, then a starving person may not merely request but may compel another to provide him with the food to which he is entitled by right. Such cases make clear the way in which the concept of a right is a stronger moral concept than that of a duty (i.e., a duty not based on a right): One person may not compel another to contribute if in failing to do so he is violating only a duty, such as the duty of benevolence. But if the omission is a violation of right, the holder of the right is permitted to use force if necessary to secure his right.

The definitions of four kinds of rights provided earlier may be suitably amended to take account of the second-order elements inherent in rights. Thus we would have:

(Rl′) X has a right$_1$ to A over against Y just in case X is at liberty with respect to A, Y has a duty not to interfere with X's doing or having A, and X is at liberty to use appropriate means if necessary to prevent Y from interfering with his or her doing or having A.

Definitions (R2), (R3), and (R4) may be revised similarly. Each of the four senses of "having a right" entails having a second-order right to protect the holder of the right in its exercise and to demand from others the progressively stronger obligations which the four types of rights impose.

The second-order right to protect rights is itself a right$_1$, since it imposes on others a duty not to interfere with the right-holder's efforts to protect his right. Perhaps it also includes a right$_2$ that others not deprive the right-holder of the means which he needs to use to protect his right. Possibly there are even some cases in which the protection of one person's rights is so urgent, and the right-holder's ability to act so limited, that others have a duty not to refuse assistance, or a positive duty to assist, in protecting the right. Possibly, in other words, some second-order rights, in some circumstances, are rights$_3$ or rights$_4$. The character of the second-order right, like the means which it justifies, will vary with the importance of the first-order right in question.[8]

My right to harvest and eat the crops I have grown on my land, for example, is a right$_1$. I am morally entitled to do so, and others may not interfere. But others have no consequent duty to assist me, and so this right is not a right$_3$ or a right$_4$. My right entails a second-order right to remove from my property anyone who steals my corn. This second-order right is itself a right$_1$: it does not create a duty in anyone to assist me in throwing the interloper off my land.[9] But in the case of an even more basic right the situation may be different. If someone tries to kill me, I may not only fight him off myself but may also call on another person to assist me. The second-order right to protect one's right to life seems to be a right$_3$.[10]

The means appropriate for the defense of the right must be gauged according to the seriousness of the right threatened. Basic human rights, which are applications of the right of all persons to self-determination, are rights in whose defense we may justifiably employ force or coercion if necessary. Several such rights have been mentioned: the right to freedom of expression and of religious practice, the right to freedom of the person, and the right to life are examples of such basic human rights. But I make no claim to have provided an exhaustive list of such rights, or one which is free from controversy. As a result there is an element of vagueness in the defense which has been provided for the use of force in defense of rights. Whether force or coercion is justified in defense of property or in securing an adequate level of welfare, for example, depends in part on whether property rights and welfare rights are granted the status of basic human rights, essential expressions of the right to self-determination.

But this vagueness is necessary and proper. Different political views include different lists of rights among basic human rights, and they therefore support differing accounts of when force may be used in their protection. Theorists and politicians who place particular emphasis on property rights and others who put greater stress on welfare rights are likely to disagree on the justifiability of force in particular contexts. Nevertheless both parties to such disputes can agree that rights provide a moral defense for the employment of force or coercion.

In the present chapter and the one preceding I have tried to present the moral case both for and against coercion on the basis of a theory of rights. Our recognition of the moral status of persons commits us to certain basic rights and to an underlying general right to self-determination, I have argued. Because coercion deprives us of the freedom to determine our lives by our choices, it is prima facie a wrong against persons. However, the basic rights of persons include second-order rights to secure and protect the exercise of the rights. It is when the exercise of basic human rights is threatened that the presumption against coercion can be overcome and its employment may be morally justified.

In the last chapter the account of coercion which has been provided will be put to the test by applying it to the assessment of one of the major coercive institutions of the modern state: the institution of punishment. The analysis of coercion, and of its justification, that has been provided above will be used to explore the question of when, and under what governing principles, the institution of punishment is morally justifiable. Before turning to that extended application, however, it is necessary to spell out some of the implications of the moral status of coercion for the nature and functioning of the state in general. In the next brief chapter we turn to these topics.

Notes

1. The distinction between offers and threats is discussed in chapter 3, above. Cf. Robert Nozick, "Coercion," in Sidney Morgenbesser, Patrick Suppes, and Morton White, eds., *Philosophy, Science and Method: Essays in Honor of Ernest Nagel* (New York: St. Martin's Press, 1969), 447–53; Virginia Held, "Threats and Coercive Offers," in J. Roland Pennock and John W. Chapman, eds., *Coercion, Nomos*, vol. 14 (Chicago: Atherton Aldine Co., 1972), 49–62.

2. See Thomas Schelling, *The Strategy of Conflict* (Oxford: Oxford University Press, 1960); Gregory Kavka, "Some Paradoxes of Deterrence," *Journal of Philosophy* 75, no. 6 (June 1978): 285–302.

3. I have discussed some of the moral questions surrounding nuclear deterrence in "Threats, Intentions, and Nuclear Deterrence," in Michael Bradie and Nicholas Rescher, eds., *Bowling Green Studies in Applied Philosophy, Vol. V* (1983); in "Nuclear Politics and Christian Ethics," *Christian Scholar's Review* 12, no. 3 (1983); and, at greater length, in "The Moral Status of Nuclear Deterrence," *Social Philosophy and Policy* 3, no. 1 (Autumn 1985): 93–117.

4. For simplicity I leave out the right not to have something done to one—a $right_2$ in the account above.

5. Kant argues further than such compulsion or coercion is in no way a restriction on the other's freedom, since it serves to ensure the freedom of all. I would not describe the situation in precisely Kant's language, which seems to me to presuppose a rather special sense of "freedom." But I fully support the somewhat more modest claim, implied by Kant's account, that legitimate coercion serves on the whole to enhance rather than limit the freedom of individuals.

6. Immanuel Kant, *The Metaphysical Elements of Justice*, trans. John Ladd (Indianapolis: Bobbs-Merrill, 1965), 37.

7. "Liberties" in Hohfeld's classification do not seem to include second-order rights; this, I think, is a further reason to exclude them from the class of rights proper.

8. I have spoken only of second-order rights, but if second-order rights are rights in senses (Rl′)–(R4′) they must themselves include third-order rights. I am not sure what this might mean, however, or whether the notion is coherent: third-order rights would be rights to protect one's right to protect one's rights. And the argument for second-order rights might appear to imply an infinite series of higher-order rights. Whether we admit or deny the existence of such highly abstract rights, however, they are of no practical importance for the purposes of this study.

9. If the property rights in question are legal rights, then my second-order rights are partially or wholly assumed by the state. A police officer has a duty to assist me in evicting a trespasser—not because my right has become a right₃ but because I have transferred my second-order right₁ to the state.

10. This might seem to be an example of protecting my *life* rather than protecting my right to life. But it does not make sense to say that I have a right ₃ to life: what would it mean to call on another for assistance in living? What I need from another person in the case described is assistance in *protecting* my life, i.e., in protecting what I have a right to.

9
COERCION AND THE STATE

The present brief chapter takes up two issues which help to link the foregoing account of coercion and its moral justification to the particular issue of punishment, the topic of the last chapter. These have to do, first, with the alienability of second-order rights and, second, with the coerciveness of governmental institutions. The alienability of second-order rights which arise from natural rights can be seen as the moral basis for state institutions which employ coercion or force. And, I shall argue, it is essential to recognize the ways in which the power of the state over individuals is coercive or potentially coercive, even though the threat of legal sanctions is not usually the principal reason why most people comply with laws and rules.

The Alienability of Second-Order Rights

According to the traditional doctrine, natural rights are absolute and inalienable. I have argued above that these claims, properly understood, are correct. Natural rights also include second-order rights, however; and the second-order rights derived from natural or human rights are by no means inalienable. A person might very well decide that the most effective way to protect the exercise of his rights is to transfer to some person or institution the right to use force for their protection.

The notion of alienation or transfer of second-order rights is a key to understanding the legitimacy of government. The state may be viewed as *a system of social institutions to which individuals transfer their second-order rights to protect their rights*. This is the meaning of the doctrine that the state holds a monopoly on the legitimate use of force: in the context of the state, certain institutions have the right to use force when necessary to protect the rights of individuals, and individuals no longer have such a right, or have it subject to legal as well as moral limitations.

The right to punish violators of the law is a right which is held only by a limited number of individuals who hold specific positions in governmental institutions. And this right, whose nature and exercise I shall explore at length in the following chapter, is derived from the conferred second-order right of the state to protect rights. Ultimately, therefore, it is on the rights of individuals that the justification of the state's use of coercion and force, and of its attendant restrictions on individual rights, is founded.

This explanation of the legitimacy of coercive power does not presuppose that there must ever have been a formal, explicit transfer of second-order rights from individuals to the state. The historical social contract theorists have occasionally posited such an act as essential to the legitimacy of government, and their critics, including David Hume, have rightly dismissed this suggestion as implausible and morally irrelevant.[1] My claim is rather that to ground the exercise of coercive power in the alienated second-order rights of individuals establishes the right conceptual link between the moral protection individuals deserve and the legitimacy of governmental force. The reason why governments may properly employ force is that in doing so they protect and preserve individual rights more effectively than could individuals by their own efforts.

Needless to say, not every exercise of power can be defended in this way. In the following chapter I shall argue, for example, that individual rights impose stringent limits on the kinds and degrees of punishment that a state may properly impose. My point is that, when the coercive power of the state is legitimately employed, it is appropriate and helpful to understand that power as derived from the second-order right of individuals to protect their rights. There is, I think, nothing radically new in the substance of this suggestion—perhaps it can be understood as simply an elaboration, using the terms that have proven useful in our analysis of coercion, of the commonplace doctrine that legitimate power is based upon the consent of the governed. My purpose in proposing this link is to give further emphasis to the close logical and moral relationship between coercion and the rights of individuals.

Does the State Coerce?

But here a paradox arises from the account of coercion that has been given above. We take the state to be a paradigm example of an institution which employs coercion and claims legitimacy in doing so. But the definition that has been given of coercion calls into question whether the normal operation of the state is in fact coercive.

One of the primary functions of a state is to make and enforce laws which provide, among other benefits, protection against violation of individual rights. Governments enact and enforce laws which prohibit certain actions—laws prohibiting theft, for example. They do so with the expectation that their enactment and enforcement of the law will reduce the incidence of the proscribed acts.[2]

And laws do affect behavior: individuals usually comply with the requirements of the law. To be sure, there are exceptions. There are laws so little known or so irregularly enforced that few people obey them, and there are individuals who pay little attention to law. By and large, however, the laws which a government makes and enforces are obeyed.

The reason for compliance, it seems obvious, is the state's coercive power. But the definition of coercion which has been given in the preceding chapters seems to imply that coercion plays a much smaller role in bringing about compliance with the law than it appears to play. A person is coerced, it has been argued, when he performs an act out of fear of an intolerable harm which another has threatened to bring about if he does not. According to this definition, laws are seldom coercive, for two reasons.

In the first place, the motivation which is a criterion of coercion may not be present. To be coerced is to act in the face of a threat with a particular motivation, viz., fear of the consequences of defying the threat. But surely many of those who obey laws do so out of motives in which fear of the consequences of violation has little if any part. Compliance with the law is motivated by habit, by the example of others, by good will and recognition of the necessity of mutual restraint, and by any number of other considerations.

But let us suppose that, at least in some unusual cases, fear of the consequences is the decisive factor in motivating compliance. Even so, an individual may not be coerced, since many legal penalties are insufficient to coerce. The threat of a fine or brief imprisonment, even when the public opprobrium of conviction is taken into account, may not be a sufficiently severe threat to make commission of a crime effectively an ineligible choice of action. Threats such as these undoubtedly make the prohibited act a less attractive option than it would otherwise be. But coercion occurs only when the victim faces intolerable harm if she refuses to comply with the threat. This may occasionally be true of legal threats, depending on the crime they are attached to and the strength of a person's motives for committing it. But in most cases the harm threatened is undesirable but far from intolerable.

The coercive activity of the state, therefore, is much more limited than it at first appears. Most of us, most of the time, are not coerced to obey the law. This is not to say that coercion does not play an important role in maintaining order, or that we do not all act from time to time almost entirely out of fear of unacceptable penalties. The reason why most people pay their taxes more or less honestly, I suspect, is primarily their fear of the penalties for being detected in dishonesty. It is unreasonable to risk a prison sentence for the sake of a few hundred dollars. Yet this is not the characteristic way in which legal penalties shape our actions. Only for seriously disturbed individuals is there no reason to refrain from murder and arson except fear of the penalties if they are caught.

The same point can be supported in an indirect way by noting the consequences which would follow if laws were always or usually coercive in their effect. It has been argued above that persons deserve neither praise nor blame for actions which are performed under coercion. If laws coerce obedience, then no one deserves moral credit for obeying them, however diligently and at however great a cost. The difference between law-abiding citizens and criminals is then merely that the former regularly yield to coercive threats made by the government, while the latter manage to defy those threats on some occasions.

But of course this is not the way we normally conceive of obedience to the law. Granted, we do not lavish praise upon a person simply because on some occasion or other he has obeyed the law. But we do consider it praiseworthy, provided the laws which exist are just and fair, to obey the law scrupulously and consistently. On the other hand, we withhold commendation from a person who obeys simply out of fear of the penalty. The person who is scrupulously honest on his income tax return because his last three returns were audited and his accountant is in jail is not the kind of person we hold up as a moral example to our children.[3]

Our moral judgments concerning compliance with law, therefore, support the conclusion that the definition of coercion led to: most people, most of the time, are not coerced to obey the law. It is characteristic of legal systems, all the same, that they have coercive means at their disposal. Furthermore, even laws which are not themselves coercive are *potentially* coercive.

The potential coerciveness of every law arises from its place in a larger legal system. Characteristic of legal systems is a certain kind of escalation of penalties. The fine for overtime parking in a municipal lot might be five dollars—scarcely sufficient to coerce anyone. But failure to pay this fine by a stated deadline may lead to a twenty-dollar fine. And failure to pay this penalty is eventually punishable by more severe penalties, such as impoundment of one's automobile or imprisonment. Or, to take another example, a person who commits a

misdemeanor may face a maximum sentence of ten days' imprisonment if he is caught. This threat will likely be insufficient to coerce
compliance. But if he is arrested and fails to appear for his trial, or if
he is convicted and escapes from the prison, he will be faced with
much harsher penalties.

Behind even the mildest legal threats, therefore, stands the threat of
progressively more severe penalties for failure to comply. The threat of
even minor sanctions is in this way potentially coercive. It constitutes
noncoercive duress against a coercive background, since the threat is
made by an institution which has and exercises extensive powers of
force and coercion.

The actual infliction of punishment, moreover, is a clear instance of
coercion. When a person is imprisoned she is subjected to physical
restraints on her movements and also to coercive threats of intolerable
consequences if she attempts to escape or violates prison rules. The
armed guards stationed in towers along prison walls threaten death to
those who attempt to escape, and this coercive threat supplements
physical restraints such as locked doors and barred windows.

Other forms of punishment, less obviously, are also instances of
coercion. A court's judgment that a person convicted of a crime must
pay a fine or devote a certain number of hours to public service is
implicitly a threat to bring the full force of the law to bear on her if she
fails to do what is required. A coercive threat is therefore a part of the
court's judgment.

The actual imposition of legal sanctions does characteristically include an element of coercion. There are several reasons why the
court's requirement has greater force than the law has over our ordinary behavior. First, the threatened penalty is stiffer. To attempt to
evade a small fine may lead to a prison sentence. Second, and probably
more important, the court's threat has much greater credibility than
the threat of the law in general. The court has the offender in its
power, and it is likely to keep her under close supervision to ensure
that she carries out its directives. The ordinary citizen who must
choose whether to obey a traffic law, by contrast, faces a threat which
is not only less severe but less credible. Only a small number of those
who violate the law are apprehended, and still fewer are convicted and
punished. The likelihood of having to suffer the legal penalty for a
violation of law is therefore relatively low.

When the direct imposition of sanctions is not in question, the effect
of law upon behavior is seldom directly coercive. Its effect rather takes
the form of noncoercive duress, together with other means such as
admonition and persuasion. The enactment of laws does not affect
individuals' behavior directly; rather, this influence is mediated not
only by the institutions which enforce laws but also by parents,

employers, friends, and others who hold no office but encourage or expect obedience to law. All of these modes of influence take place against a coercive background, however, and the requirements of law are potentially coercive. The state has coercive power, and it uses this power when necessary to enforce laws.

Is Coercion the Issue?

The difference between coercion and noncoercive duress is relatively unimportant from the coercer's viewpoint, we have noted earlier in this study, despite its significance for the victim. The reason is that the coercer cannot by his actions alone make a threat coercive; rather, whether it is coercive depends on the victim's response.

This fact suggests that it may be inappropriate even to ask the general question of whether, and with what justification, the state exercises coercion. Certainly governments have the power to coerce, and they do so on many occasions. But it is only after the fact—after the threat has been made, and after the goverment's direct involvement in the threat situation is ended—that coercion can be distinguished from lesser degrees of duress.

What is really at issue, therefore, is not whether the state may coerce but, rather, whether the state may threaten serious harm and inflict harm on those who do not comply. What requires justification is not precisely the *coerciveness* of a threat but simply its *seriousness* as a threat and the extent of harm that is done if the threat is carried through. To judge whether the state exercises its power properly we must determine whether other moral considerations outweigh the costs, which include harms inflicted and the closing off by threats of options which we would prefer were left open to us.

The question of whether and when the state may coerce, then, is really a question of what harms the state may threaten and carry out for what purposes. I cannot attempt to give an answer to this question which takes into account all of the innumerable ways in which the state influences individual behavior, from fishing limits to equal opportunity laws to the military draft. In the next chapter I shall attempt to answer this question as it applies to one particular area, however: that of institutions of legal punishment.

Notes

1. On the relevance of consent for political obligation see A. John Simmons, *Moral Principles and Political Obligation* (Princeton: Princeton University Press, 1979), esp. chaps. 3–4.

2. Strictly speaking, there can be no theft in the legal sense until a law against it has been enacted, since the law defines what counts as "theft." I am using the term above, therefore, in its ordinary rather than its strictly legal sense.

3. The same point can be supported with reference to unfair laws: we do not excuse a person who complies with a grossly unfair legal requirement simply because there is a penalty attached to disobedience. We expect a person to refuse to comply with a racially discriminatory law, for example, even if doing so requires risking punishment. But if the threat of punishment were sufficient to coerce, we could not expect a person to defy it but could only hope that he might be of exceptionally strong character and hence capable of overcoming the threat.

10
THE JUSTIFICATION OF PUNISHMENT

The institution of punishment is a paradigm example of the power of the state to threaten and inflict harm, and in the present chapter I explore what justification can be given for the practice of punishment. I approach this question by considering in turn the three major defenses that have been offered for the practice of punishment, defenses grounded in considerations of rehabilitation, deterrence, and retribution. To each there are serious moral objections, grounded in each case in the rights of individuals which have been explored in previous chapters. We seem therefore to be led to the conclusion that punishment cannot be morally justified. But this conclusion, I shall argue, does not give proper weight to individual desert in the distribution of social benefits and burdens. When questions of justice and desert are taken into account, punishment can be defended morally— but only on the condition that certain of its central features be retributive rather than deterrent or rehabilitative.

Theories of Punishment

Punishment in the legal sense consists in the deliberate deprivation of rights or infliction of hard treatment on individuals by the recognized authorities of a state.[1] In the philosophical literature concerning punishment we find three distinct positions concerning its justifiability, which we may call in a loose sense distinct theories of punishment: the deterrent, rehabilitative, and retributive theories. Other positions than these are possible, needless to say, but these three exhaust the theories of punishment that have been systematically developed by philosophers (and are frequently encountered in other contexts as well). For the purposes of this study I assume that if punishment is justified it is justified for one of these three sets of reasons.

The *deterrent* theory of punishment holds that punishment is justified by its effect in discouraging the person punished and others from committing future offenses similar to that for which the punishment is inflicted.[2] A purpose closely related to deterrence is the *incapacitation* of the person punished, rendering him incapable, either temporarily or permanently, of repeating his offense.[3] Capital punishment is the most permanent and effective means of incapacitation; but imprisonment also disables a person temporarily from committing most crimes. According to the deterrent theory, of which I take incapacitation as a particular application, punishment is justified by the socially useful effects of deterrence and incapacitation of known criminals and potential criminals. Its application and severity should therefore be set in such a way as to achieve these ends effectively and economically.

In contrast, the *rehabilitative* or reformative view of punishment sees the purpose of punishment above all in its beneficial effects on the individual. Criminal acts are taken to be symptoms of malfunction or maladjustment of the person who commits them; and the treatment of criminals, on this view, should aim at restoring them to psychological health and making their behavior conform to socially acceptable standards. Although I have referred to the rehabilitative view as a theory of punishment, what it proposes is not so much a defense of punishment as a substitute for it, since treatment of lawbreakers for therapeutic ends lacks some of the characteristic features of punishment. On this view, each criminal should be subjected to the treatment which will most effectively restore his mental health or improve his behavior.[4]

The deterrent theory of punishment is frequently supported by a utilitarian theory of ethics. A justified system of punishment, according to the utilitarian standard, is one which brings about the greatest net benefit to all, and a system of punishment which is acceptable on utilitarian grounds will balance the harm caused to those who are punished against the harm to others which is thereby prevented.[5]

It is possible to defend deterrence apart from a utilitarian moral theory: one might advocate, for example, that punishment be set in such as way as to maximize deterrence, regardless of its contribution to the suffering of criminals. But without the upper limit which is set by utilitarianism, this would lead to extremely harsh punishments, since increasing the severity of the penalty for a crime is always likely to bring about at least a slight further decrease in its incidence. Surely some limit must be set, on moral grounds, for the severity of punishment that can be applied for the sake of deterrence. The utilitarian standard of minimizing overall suffering seems to set this limit in a plausible way, and for this reason I shall assume that the deterrent defense of punishment rests on a utilitarian foundation.

The deterrent and rehabilitative theories have arisen as reactions against the traditional *retributive* defense of punishment, which holds that the justification of punishment lies in its exacting retribution for the offense committed. Retributivism asserts that the person who has committed a crime deserves to be punished accordingly. This account of punishment, unlike the others, is backward-looking: it judges the appropriateness of punishment by the offense that a person has committed, not by the expected effects of his punishment on himself or on society. Among the essential features of a retributive system of punishment which will be discussed more fully below are the requirements of responsibility for the act punished and of proportionality between offense and penalty.[6]

Alternative Ends

Pace Aristotle, the philosophical debate about the justification of punishment is largely taken up with deliberation concerning ends. On the rehabilitative view, the end of punishment (or its substitute) should be the healing or improvement of the offender. According to the deterrent view, its aim should be to prevent crime. According to the retributive theory, the purpose of punishment should be paying back the offense. The topic of the present chapter is which of these ends, if any, can be adopted as the purpose of punishment and can justify the threat and imposition of legal sanctions.

Several assumptions should be explicitly acknowledged before proceeding. First, I am assuming that both punishment and crime cause suffering to those on whom they are imposed. To be subjected to the legal deprivations of punishment—imprisonment, fines, work requirements, or the like—is to suffer certain important kinds of harm. Equally obviously, to be the victim of crime is to suffer harm, whether it be physical injury or financial loss. For simplicity I shall refer to all of these harms as kinds of suffering.

Second, I am assuming throughout that punishment does, all else being equal, prevent crime. This is not a conceptual but an empirical claim; it is, in simplest terms, the assumption that threats work. Human motivation is such that the threat of undesirable consequences for performing an act discourages those who are threatened from performing the act. This assumption, I think, is quite safe. It might have been false, of course, if human nature were differently constituted. But if this assumption were false there would be no such thing as a threat and no point in punishing.

Turning now to the alternative ends that have been proposed, let us consider first the rehabilitative view. The recommendation that traditional forms of punishment should be eliminated in favor of psychological treatment of criminals is one that is widely supported by social scientists and by the public, and it is frequently urged by advocates of prison reform. A particularly forceful statement of the view has been given by a psychologist, James V. McConnell:

> I foresee the day when we [will be able to] convert the worst criminal into a decent, respectable citizen in a matter of a few months—or perhaps even less time than that. . . .
> We should try to regulate human conduct by offering rewards for good behavior whenever possible instead of threatening punishment for breaches of the law. We should reshape our society so that we would all be trained from birth to do what society wants us to do. We have the techniques now to do it. Only by using them can we hope to maximize human potentiality. . . . We'd assume that a felony was clear evidence that the criminal had somehow acquired full-blown social neurosis and needed to be cured, not punished. We'd send him to a rehabilitation center where he'd undergo positive brainwashing until we were quite sure he had become a law-abiding citizen who would not again commit an antisocial act. We'd probably have to restructure his entire personality.[7]

The moral objections to the substitution of rehabilitation for punishment—whether advocated in such an uncompromising manner as this or in some more modest form—are evident. They have been explored frequently in philosophical discussions, and I shall mention them only briefly here.[8]

What is most fundamentally wrong with substituting treatment for punishment is that to do so is to fail to respect persons as persons. Rehabilitation divorces treatment of individuals radically from their choices, since liability to rehabilitative measures is dependent not on a person's past acts but on his predicted future behavior. But the ability of individuals to make choices which affect them and to carry these choices out is essential to the moral standing of persons, as has been argued in our earlier account of natural rights. Compulsory treatment for all criminals therefore systematically undermines the moral standing of persons by undertaking, in McConnell's terms, to "restructure" an individual's "entire personality."

The quotation above, needless to say, represents an extreme form of the rehabilitative ideal. McConnell recommends that we "combine sensory deprivation with drugs, hypnosis, and astute manipulation of reward and punishment to gain almost absolute control over an individual's behavior."[9] Other defenders of the rehabilitative view would restrict the means of treatment to more humane methods, but the ultimate end is the same.

The force of the objection to such treatment is not diminished by advocating more modest means, for the question is primarily one of ends. May the institutions of punishment compel individuals to submit to psychological treatment intended to shape their future behavior? The moral status of persons and the importance of their rights require a negative answer.

The problem with this view is not that the end which it proposes is indefensible or intrinsically immoral. The problem is rather that this is an end which must not be imposed on persons by coercive means. There is nothing wrong with making treatment of many kinds, including behavior modification by Skinnerian means, available to individuals who desire it and undergo the treatment voluntarily. There is even a place for compulsory treatment of some. Without question there are persons who violate the law because of mental disease or incapacity. Such persons ought to be given treatment and, if they pose a danger to others, ought to be confined until they are able to take responsibility for their actions. But these are precisely the circumstances that invalidate a person's right to be treated as a person. A psychopath is not fully a moral person, since he lacks the capacity to take responsibility for his acts, and he ought not to be accorded the full range of rights due to persons.

The rehabilitative view would include *all* legal offenders in this category, taking the simple act of committing a serious crime as sufficient evidence of mental disease. But crimes may be committed, after all, consciously and deliberately, by persons in full control of their actions and in full knowledge of what they are doing. On the rehabilitative view, even such deliberate acts are evidence of psychological or sociological disease of some sort. But this is absurd. The fact of having committed a crime is by no means adequate evidence that a person lacks normal capacities and hence has forfeited his rights to be treated as a responsible agent.

But, the defender of the retributive view may reply, surely a system of treatment for criminals is preferable to a system of conventional punishment. And if punishment is morally defensible—if we may inflict suffering on individuals simply because they have violated the law—why may we not substitute for punishment forms of treatment whose purpose is not to cause suffering but to benefit the criminal? Is it morally worse to benefit a criminal than to harm him, if the program of treatment is as effective in deterring crime?

It may be noted, first, that one who defends the rehabilitative view along these lines is adopting a far more modest goal than have most defenders of this view, if treatment is to be imposed only on those who have already violated the law. Indeed, McConnell and many others have suggested that a principal advantage of the rehabilitative program is that it can be imposed on individuals before they commit a crime—imposed on those judged likely to commit crimes in the future, perhaps imposed through conditioning programs on everyone. Restriction of treatment to those who are genuinely guilty of crimes would greatly diminish the scope of the rehabilitative vision.

Second, even though it is doubtless true that programs of reform are in many cases sincerely intended to serve the good of their subjects, the standard by which benefit is determined is inevitably set by those who impose the treatment, regardless of whether the subject accepts the same standard. Criminals must be led to accept normal goals and normal means of achieving them, on this view. Those who have deliberately chosen to flout the accepted standards of normality in social behavior must be subjected to therapeutic programs which will bring them into conformity with the rest of society.

Even if we assume that those in charge of rehabilitative institutions have the purest of intentions—they genuinely want to help criminals, not merely to keep society running efficiently—the power which they are granted is an extremely dangerous one. The moral objection against granting anyone power of this kind may be seen most clearly, perhaps, in the case of conscientious disobedience to a law which the violator believes to be unjust. A person who deliberately violates a law, believing the law to be unjust and intending by her violation to draw public attention to its injustice, may justly be punished for her offense. Many defenders of civil disobedience have envisioned suffering the legal penalty as part of their intended action, as a way of demonstrating their seriousness and good faith. Reasons might be given for withholding punishment in some such cases, and yet no injustice is done if it is imposed.[10] But punishment defended on rehabilitative grounds—treatment with the intent of correcting the abnormality shown by the act or of preventing the individual from committing similar acts in the future—is clearly unjust and an affront to the integrity of the person.

We ought not to grant anyone the power to subject violators of unjust laws to compulsory treatment intended to restore them to "normality," therefore. And the example of conscientious disobedience suggests the grave abuses to which such power is liable even in a just society. The treatment of political dissidents in the Soviet Union and in Argentina during the recent period of military rule provides chilling examples of the abuses to which such power can be put.

The reform of criminals, therefore, cannot be the end of punishment. There is a need for rehabilitative institutions in society, but their purpose and operation must be quite different from those of the institutions of punishment. To mistake one kind of institution for the other is a profound and dangerous error.

Deterrence and Retribution: An Apparent Dilemma

Considerations such as these, I believe, invalidate rehabilitation as a general aim for institutions of punishment. Let us turn to the other two theories of punishment, which defend punishment on deterrent and on retributive grounds.

The question of the justification of punishment, it has been observed, is a question primarily of ends. We want to know what ends may morally be pursued by means of legal punishment. The retributivist's answer to the question of ends is that punishment ought to repay the offense, to bring about a balance of wrong done with the suffering imposed. On the retributive view, the end of the practice of punishment is to impose suffering on appropriate persons and to the proper degree.

But, we want to object, is causing suffering the sole purpose of punishment? Does it have no purpose except to cause a certain kind of harm? The deterrent position appears much more attractive: the end of punishment is claimed to be not the *imposition* of suffering but its *prevention*. One person's punishment is justified by its effect in deterring others, and also in incapacitating him, from imposing even greater suffering. To forbear to punish offenders would lead only to even greater suffering in the long run.

In discussing the end of punishment, therefore, the deterrent theory appears much more attractive than retributivism. Where the retributive theory seems to assert that an evil—the imposition of suffering on offenders—is in itself good, the deterrent view understands the evil only as a means to a good.

Yet deterrence can justify certain kinds of punishment that are clearly unjust. Consider exemplary punishment, for example, which consists either of punishment of persons known to be innocent or exceptionally harsh treatment of the guilty in order to provide a public example. There is no doubt that such treatment can be a highly effective deterrent to crime, and it has been employed in some legal systems. The deterrent view of punishment would seem not merely to permit but to require that we employ exemplary punishment in cases where less severe measures prove ineffectual in preventing some serious crime. But such harsh treatment for the sake of public example would fly in the face of justice. Justice requires that we treat persons as persons, having the full range of moral rights to self-determination and

freedom from arbitrary interference. Exemplary punishment, whatever its effectiveness as a deterrent, violates these rights.[11]

If the purpose of punishment is retribution, on the other hand,
exemplary punishment can never be justified. It makes no sense to
speak of punishing a person, as the retributivist understands the word,
for an offense which he did not commit, and it is never morally
permissible to punish a person more severely than his offense would
warrant for the sake of deterrence. Punishment must be determined
by what the person has done, not by what others will do as a result of
his treatment; it must be proportional to the crime, not to the public's
need for an example. The point of punishment is simply to punish
offenders, not to influence others.

Here we seem to face a dilemma. A basic requirement of morality is
the duty of benevolence, the duty we have to do good rather than
harm to others. And only the deterrent justification of punishment
seems consistent with our duty to do good. But recognition of individual rights is an equally basic moral requirement. And it appears that
only a retributive system of punishment gives due weight to individual
rights not to be treated arbitrarily or unfairly. Benevolence admits
only a deterrent defense for punishment, and fairness admits only a
retributive defense. Since each of these proposed ends for punishment
excludes the other, the moral principles of benevolence and fairness,
taken together, seem to lead to the conclusion that the institution of
punishment cannot be justified.

This apparent dilemma has motivated some philosophers to distinguish between two levels of justification of the institution of punishment. Thus H. L. A. Hart has distinguished between the question of
what should be the "general justifying aim" of punishment and the
question of what principles should govern distribution: the deterrent
theory, he argues, gives the best answer to the former question, while
retributive considerations must be called on to answer the latter.[12]

Useful though this maneuver appears in resolving the dilemma I
have mentioned, at bottom it only evades the central issue. For we are
asking not two questions but one: what justifies punishing people?
There is no point in offering a general justification of the existence of
an institution if the reasons offered are insufficient to justify its
operation. The question of the aim of punishment must be faced more
directly, I believe, than the two-stage account of punishment suggests.

It does not seem to me to be a satisfactory solution to attempt to
seize both horns of this dilemma, therefore, and apply them to distinct
questions concerning punishment. As a means toward a more satisfactory resolution, consider the alternative to accepting either of the two
theories of punishment—the beast, metaphorically speaking, who

stands behind the horns of the dilemma and forces us to choose. For if neither deterrence nor retribution is a morally acceptable general aim for punishment, the former for reasons of fairness and the latter for reasons of benevolence, and if there is no other alternative general defense of punishment except rehabilitation, which is equally unacceptable, then we are forced to conclude that the institution of punishment is not justified after all.

The Consequences of Eliminating Punishment

Consider the implications of this position in concrete terms. If there is no moral justification of punishment, then those who violate the law (assuming, for the moment, that there can be laws without an institution of punishment) may not be subjected to enforced hard treatment.

There are, of course, alternatives to punishment. Punishment typically involves both direct deprivation and the coercive threat of more severe deprivation: a prisoner is sentenced to a year's imprisonment but knows that refusal to serve his sentence, or attempting to escape once he has begun serving it, will lead to a much harsher penalty. The threat of punishment may coerce obedience, and even if the threat is insufficient to coerce it takes place against a coercive background.

A society which does not employ legal punishment might employ any of a number of other means of influencing individuals to comply with the law. Perhaps wide-ranging and pervasive means of persuasion and suggestion might be employed—posters on every street corner and broadcast messages over every radio station.

The obvious objection to such a substitution of persuasion for punishment is that it simply won't work. Persuasion will not bring about a high level of compliance with the law, and self-interested reasons for crime will frequently override whatever general sentiment favoring obedience a propaganda campaign might create.

But there is a deeper objection to the substitution of persuasion for punishment. In a society without an institution of legal punishment, the entire cost of crime is borne by its victims. The choice of who shall bear the burdens of crime is made, in effect, by those who commit crimes, and its burdens fall entirely on the victims of crime. By foregoing the application of punishment, the state refrains from imposing any additional suffering on criminals. Since the elimination of punishment inevitably brings about a higher incidence of crime, the state thereby permits a greater amount of suffering to be imposed on crime victims.

It seems safe to assume that, on balance, institutions of punishment prevent more suffering than they inflict. But the quantity of suffering is unimportant. Suppose, for the sake of argument, that punishment causes precisely as much suffering as it prevents, or even somewhat less. It would still be better to have an institution of punishment than not—better because the distribution of suffering would be fairer and less arbitrary.[13] The suffering that individuals incur through punishment is less objectionable than the suffering caused by crime.

Still, it might be said, punishment deters crime only at the cost of imposing a deliberate and calculated kind of suffering. To undertake to punish offenders is morally worse than allowing victims to suffer because it is worse to inflict deliberate harm than to permit another to inflict harm. The infliction of punishment involves gross infringements of the offender's right to self-determination and non-interference, and these infringements are at least comparable in seriousness with the criminal's violation of his victim's right.

To raise this objection to punishment, however, is to overlook the place of punishment as an instrument for the defense of rights. Each individual has the right to make choices and to be free from others' interference in carrying out her choices; moreover, she has the right to employ force if necessary in protecting those rights. By means of the threat of punishment, the state undertakes to provide protection for individual rights, and its moral license to employ such a threat is derived from the second-order rights of individuals. In threatening and imposing punishment, therefore, the state has a moral defense based upon individual rights. No such considerations defend the criminal's assault on the rights of the victim.

The example of a society without punishment makes it clear that none of the alternative ends that have been discussed is fully acceptable. The purpose of punishment is not simply to diminish the quantity of suffering; rather, punishment *brings about a fair distribution of the burdens of social life.* When less effective and noncoercive means are substituted for punishment, the suffering caused by crime—the cost, we might say, of the human tendency to put self-interest ahead of others' interests—is borne entirely by the victims of crime.

A just institution of punishment, in contrast, is able to place a large share of that burden where it belongs: on those who violate the law and cause suffering to others. Punishment imposes suffering on some in order to diminish the suffering caused to others. And the advantage of punishment over its absence is that the burdens of crime are placed to a greater degree on those who deserve to bear them.

This argument relies on an important and far-reaching assumption: that *those who violate the law deserve to suffer.* The end of punishment, I have said, is a just distribution of the burdens of crime, and justice is served when the imposition of suffering on the criminal reduces the suffering of the victim of crime.

Clearly, to accept this assumption is to land squarely in the retributivist camp, since we are speaking not simply of the result achieved by punishment but of imposing suffering according to individual desert. From a utilitarian point of view this should have no bearing: we ought to impose punishment in whatever way will minimize the total amount of suffering caused to all. But the problem with the utilitarian account of punishment is precisely that it makes no distinction between criminal and victim in deciding how to apportion burdens and benefits. It does make a difference who bears the burden, we want to reply: it is worse for the victim of crime to suffer than for a person guilty of a crime to suffer.

To say this is not to accept the strong retributivist view that the suffering caused to offenders is intrinsically good. There is no reason to call the suffering of criminals, or anyone's suffering or deprivation, positively good. Rather, the assumption which underlies the preceding argument is that, when suffering can be imposed on either the victim or the criminal, it is morally better to impose it on the criminal.[14]

The answer to the question of why a particular individual ought to be punished, then, is that he *deserves* punishment, because he has committed a crime and because failure to punish him will indirectly tend to increase the suffering caused to undeserving victims of crime. The only satisfactory resolution of the dilemma posed by the conflict between retributive and deterrence accounts of punishment, I believe, is to accept this much of the retributive position. The deterrent justification of punishment, in contrast, does not distinguish between the suffering caused to those who deserve it and the suffering caused to those who do not deserve it.

The crucial assumption which underlies the preceding argument is that the acts which are proscribed by law are acts which cause suffering, and that making and enforcing laws against these acts will diminish their incidence. Whether these acts are morally wrong is irrelevant, and I do not assume, as do many retributivists, that punishment is a moral repayment for wrong acts. An act need not be immoral to be legitimately proscribed. It must, however, be an act which it is permissible to close off by threats. It must not, in other words, fall within the range of actions which our basic freedom as persons entitles us to choose. Speaking our thoughts and feelings freely to others may cause them intense suffering, but we are not for that reason willing to accept laws restricting our expression. We expect, as one of our basic personal rights, to be permitted to speak our minds freely. Building a house within twenty feet of the lot line, on the other hand, is in no way immoral; yet, because we recognize the harm that can be done to all if property owners are free to build as they please anywhere on their property, we accept planning and zoning laws which impose such requirements.

The importance of desert in apportioning the costs of crime is grounded in the standing of each individual as a moral person. A person, it has been argued in chapter 7, above, is entitled to freedom from others' interference with her making and carrying out choices. The imposition of unwanted suffering by others deprives a person of this freedom. But there is a morally significant difference between suffering imposed arbitrarily, without regard for an individual's previous actions, and suffering which is imposed as a result of the person's actions. Suffering of the latter kind, though undesired, is connected with the victim's decisions, since she could have avoided it by refraining from the action which led to it.

Punishment is connected in this way with the actions of the person who is punished; and so, of course, is the carrying out of any threat. But the threat of punishment is unlike other threats in that its purpose is to protect the individual's exercise of her rights as a person. The threat of punishment—if it is part of a system of just laws which uphold individual rights—is intended to prevent infringements of rights. Moreover, when the threat fails to achieve this, punishment itself is imposed as a necessary part of the system of effective threats. When a person is punished for violating another's rights, therefore, the suffering which she undergoes is part of a system whose intent is the protection of everyone's rights, including even hers. Therefore suffering of this kind is not inconsistent with the moral status of the person punished; indeed, it is intended to preserve that moral status.

Yet there is no reason to accept the further claim of some defenders of retributive punishment that punishment is in itself good, apart from its deterrent effect. The deterrence theory is right in asserting that, if punishment had no deterrent effect, its imposition would not be justified. But the deterrent theory is wrong to conclude from this that deterrence is the end of punishment. The end of punishment is not deterrence, but a just apportionment of the costs of crime.

The lesson to be drawn from the example of eliminating punishment is this: if there were no institution of punishment, the distribution of the burdens of crime would be unjust. Given the facts of human motivation and scarcity of desired goods, social interactions will inevitably impose suffering on some. In a society without punishment the suffering imposed by interpersonal violence, for example, will fall entirely on its victims. But this is unjust, since their suffering is in no way a result of their own actions and choices, and they do not in any sense deserve to suffer. Those who inflict suffering on them, on the other hand, have made a deliberate choice to inflict suffering. It is impossible to turn their own intentions directly back on them—they cannot be made the victims of their own crime. But it is possible to reduce the suffering caused to victims of violence by imposing certain costs and burdens on those who inflict it, and this is precisely what an institution of punishment attempts to do. The end which is served by punishment, therefore, is not simply prevention of violence but a fair distribution of its costs.

A Noncoercive System of Deterrence

The need to call on retributive considerations of desert can be made clearer by considering other ways of achieving the end of deterrence. The foregoing argument for a fundamentally retributive understanding of the place of punishment can be given further support by imagining how this might be accomplished.

So far we have considered only a noncoercive system of persuasion and exhortation, and I have argued that this would be ineffective as a deterrent and would therefore leave victims to bear the full costs of crime. But modern police states have demonstrated that there are far more effective means of bringing about compliance. The methods of indoctrination, intimidation, and surveillance employed by such states to prevent the commission of crimes are extensive, and vast new opportunities for such supervision and control are opened by electronic technology.

Imagine that a well-organized and humane police state created such effective means of intimidation and surveillance that scarcely anyone ever committed a crime. Perhaps each citizen is fitted with a tiny radio-transmitted collar, of the kind that have been attached to wolves and whooping cranes, which relays his location and activities to the precinct station at all times. Anyone who is suspected of engaging in illegal activities is immediately warned to stop by the voice of a police officer (or, if this turns out to be more effective, by the taped voice of his mother) issuing from the receiver portion of his collar. If the person refuses to stop, a team of officers is at his side almost instantly to hold him securely until he satisfies them that he no longer has any intention of committing a crime. An electric shock device might be an optional accessory for emergency use.

Under such a system hardly anyone would ever succeed in committing a crime. The deterrent purpose of punishment would thus be accomplished very effectively. Other influences besides the threat of punishment would reduce the incidence of crime to an extremely low level, thus satisfying the demand which led us above to choose a system of punishment over the elimination of punishment. Moreover, the number of successful criminals to be dealt with would be so small that their treatment would have little effect on others' behavior. Perhaps, therefore, out of mercy the officials of such a state will simply let anyone who succeeded in committing a crime go free, confident that neither he nor anyone else is likely to succeed in committing another in the future. (Perhaps the electric shock unit would now be activated.) Indeed, if the officials are utilitarians they must let him go free unless punishing him would cause a further reduction in crime sufficient to outweigh the suffering of the punished.

Such a humane police state would achieve the goal of deterrence— *viz.*, reducing the incidence of crime—even more effectively than would any imaginable system of punishment. Deterrent considerations would therefore suggest that we eliminate punishment in favor of such a system. Perhaps a system as elaborate as the one I have sketched is not yet possible; but then we have all the more reason to work on developing the necessary technology rather than squander our time arresting and punishing criminals.[15]

What is wrong with our kindly totalitarian state, of course, is that it achieves deterrence only by trampling on everyone's rights, such as the right to privacy and to freedom of the person. The reason why we would choose a system of punishment over a police state without punishment is that we want to reduce the incidence of crime only in ways that respect the integrity of individuals. A system such as the one just sketched would impose a considerable cost on everyone, making every word and every movement subject to observation by the police. It would prevent crime only by imposing on all of us burdens which we do not want and do not deserve.

It is evident, then, that considerations of individual liberty rule out some highly effective ways of ensuring compliance with the law. It is better—because it is less of an invasion of our rights to liberty and self-determination—to achieve moderately high compliance through the threat of punishment than to secure nearly perfect compliance through strict behavioral control. Consideration of this example does not directly support the retributive over the deterrent justification of punishment, but it does demonstrate that deterrence, by whatever means achieved, is not the sole end of punishment.

Procedural Safeguards

The grounding of punishment in desert requires strict procedural safeguards in the actual imposition of legal penalties, for to punish a person if there is any doubt concerning his guilt is to impose an undeserved and unjustifiable harm. Such safeguards are of several kinds. There are restrictions on the manner in which evidence of criminal activity may be obtained, such as prohibitions of unreasonable search and seizure and the inadmissibility of confessions obtained under duress. Other requirements specify the strength and the nature of the evidence required for conviction, such as the requirement that the guilt of the accused not merely be the most probable explanation of the evidence presented but be proven beyond reasonable doubt. Another important protection is the *mens rea* requirement, which requires that the accused be shown to have intended to perform the illegal act of which he is accused. Acts performed unintentionally, under compulsion, or while insane are exempt from punishment under this requirement, drawn from the maxim of English common law, *actus non facit reum nisi mens sit rea*.[16]

Some of these protections may be defended on the basis of their effectiveness in deterring crime. To admit forced confessions, for example, might diminish our motivation to obey the law, since coercion can make an innocent man confess to a crime he has not committed. Doing away with this protection would make obeying the law a less reliable means of staying out of prison.

But many of the other procedural safeguards cannot be so defended. Consider the *mens rea* requirement, for example. It might be argued that this requirement assures all of us that acts we cannot avoid and are not aware of doing will not render us liable to be punished. This is an assurance we all desire, and therefore utilitarian considerations support this protection. But there is a cost attached also: the existence of such a safeguard for the innocent makes it possible for some to commit crimes and escape punishment by falsely claiming not to have met the *mens rea* requirement. To adopt a utilitarian system of punishment is to take the risk that, should procedural safeguards such as this prove at some point to cost more than they are worth in the benefits they bring about, the safeguards will be abolished.

But because we want punishment to be inflicted only on those who deserve it, retention of this protection should not be conditional on its effect on the crime rate. An individual can be deserving of punishment only if she is responsible for her act. No one deserves punishment for an unintentional act, and hence the *mens rea* requirement is essential.

Proportionality

The reason which justifies an institution of punishment, by comparison with a noncoercive system or a system of direct behavioral control, is the requirement of justice that suffering be imposed when possible on those who deserve it rather than on those who do not. Considerations of desert also support another basic element of the retributive theory of punishment, that of *proportionality* between offense and penalty. The more serious a crime has been committed, the more serious ought to be the penalty imposed for its commission.

A retributive theory of punishment need not specify a cardinal scale of seriousness of offenses and punishments—it need not attempt to specify how many years' imprisonment is required by an armed robbery. What is essential is that there be an ordinal ranking of seriousness of crimes and severity of penalties and a mapping of offenses onto punishments in order of severity. Judgments of the severity of offenses and of sanctions, it should be noted, will make reference to rights: the more serious offenses are those which more seriously infringe the rights of others, and the more severe penalties are those which involve farther-reaching and longer-lasting deprivations of rights.

The retributive theory of punishment, as I understand it, does not propose an exact matching of punishment to offense but is rather a *constraint on the reasons* for imposing one penalty rather than another in a particular case. A particular penalty must be justified by the seriousness of the offense. Different societies, and the same society at different times, are likely to have widely different scales and kinds of punishment. What retributivism demands is that, at a given time in a society, the imposition of a punishment of greater severity on one offender than on another be justified by the greater seriousness of the offense committed. In contrast, deterrent considerations would judge the appropriateness of penalties by their expected effectiveness in reducing the incidence of crime.

The standard of severity employed in such judgments must be a standard of perceived severity, since no objective standard is available by which a society can determine the true severity either of offense or of punishment. In this sense the basis of punishment is subjective and relativistic, and retributive considerations do not prevent wide variation in the punishment meted out for similar offenses in different societies or in different periods. This variation is avoidable only by invoking a universal and objective moral standard as the basis of judgments of seriousness; but if any such standard exists it is by no means universally accepted. The judgments of seriousness must therefore represent a consensus of seriousness as perceived by the members of the society in question. The fact that in eighteenth-century England murder was punished by hanging while in modern England it is punished by imprisonment does not in itself violate the standards of justice in apportioning punishment. But a country which imprisons murderers and hangs thieves would violate those requirements. The retributive standard is one of comparative proportionality.

Yet there is more to be said than this: even a retributive theory weaker than full-blown moral retributivism can set at least some outer cardinal limits on the severity of punishments in addition to the comparative requirement that has been mentioned. What has been said so far might give the impression that there is nothing unjust about a scale of punishments which imposes a ten-dollar fine for murder and lesser fines for everything else. Nor, if the relative proportionality is preserved, would there seem to be any reasons of justice for choosing between such a system and one which imposes death for overtime parking and ranges up to slow and painful death by torture for more serious offenses.

It is possible, if unlikely, that either of these might be defended on other grounds: a very lenient system or a very cruel system might prove to be the most effective and economical way of securing deterrence or, for that matter, rehabilitation of the offender. Whether this is true depends on empirical facts about human behavior. But neither of these systems, surely, can be defended as imposing on the criminal the suffering that he deserves to bear. Although retributive considerations do not assign a single appropriate penalty for a particular act, whatever the social circumstances, they do rule out systems which fall outside of what could sensibly be defended as the appropriate penalty for crime. And, given the assumption of the retributive theory that punishment must be deserved by the offense, neither a fine for murder nor execution for a parking violation can possibly be defended. Nor—to cite two factual examples—can retributive principles condone the sentencing of political activist John Sinclair to ten years' imprisonment for possession of two marijuana cigarettes or the absolution of former president Nixon from any punishment for abuse of high office. The objections to both overly harsh and overly lenient punishments are obvious: to punish with excessive severity is to impose on offenders a harm greater than they deserve to suffer, thus unjustly increasing the costs of crime; while to punish too leniently will result, as will foregoing punishment altogether, in a greater share of the costs falling on innocent victims of crime.

Conclusion: Punishment as Justified Coercion

In sum, the retributive account of punishment seems to offer the only acceptable justification for punishment, and only this defense is consistent with the rights of the individuals to whom it is applied. The use of coercion, and of threats against a coercive background, by institutions of government is justified as a means of defending individual rights, and the legitimacy of governmental force is derived from individuals' authorization of the government to exercise their second-order rights. But an institution of punishment whose primary end is either rehabilitation or deterrence fails to give adequate respect to the rights of individuals; and the same charge can be made against either a noncoercive system of persuasion or a strict system of behavioral control.

In answering the question, "What justifies us in punishing this person?", we must appeal not to his own presumed good nor to the good of society as a whole. Rather, we must defend each application of punishment as necessary to bring about a fair distribution of the overall burdens of crime.[17] And a fair distribution is a distribution which apportions suffering, whenever possible, to those who deserve to suffer rather than to those who do not. Those who are guilty of crimes deserve to be punished; a fair system of punishment, therefore, will punish only those who are genuinely guilty of crimes. Other goals, ranging from the general improvement of society to the improvement of the individual, must be subordinate to the end of just and fair apportionment of the costs of crime.

The particular case of punishment, which has been the subject of this chapter, illustrates the relationship between the moral notions of coercion and rights which have been discussed in earlier chapters. For punishment poses forcefully the central question of when and why coercion can be justified. Coercion, it has been argued, consists in causing another to act by overriding all other considerations with the threat of intolerable harm, and such an intervention into an individual's behavior violates the right each person has, as a moral person, to choose and act freely and without interference by others. But the same rights to free choice and action carry with them second-order rights to protect their exercise with force or the threat of force when necessary. And it is in the exercise of these second-order rights, above all, that coercion can sometimes be justified.

Institutions of punishment are paradigm examples of coercive structures. The application of punishment involves both force and the threat of force, and, even though the threat of punishment is not a severe enough threat to constitute coercion in most cases, such a threat is made against a clearly coercive background. The institution of punishment, therefore, requires a moral justification sufficient to override its interference with the rights of individuals. I have argued in the present chapter that neither the absence of any system of punishment nor a system whose basic features are designed to achieve the goal of deterrence or reform gives sufficient weight to the rights of the individuals who are affected. A retributive system, because it justifies punishment not merely by its effectiveness in securing some social goal but also by the merit of those punished, is better able than either of the alternatives to give due recognition to the rights of all to self-determination and noninterference. Retributive considerations therefore mandate certain features of the institution of punishment, such as the *mens rea* requirement and a principle of proportionality, even if their elimination would enhance the deterrent or rehabilitative effects of punishment.

Similar considerations can be applied to other instances of the use of coercion. It is clear, for example, that the use of coercion simply as a means of achieving individual ends—threatening severe harm unless a person gives me his money or carries out some distasteful task for me—cannot be justified by arguments such as those that have been given for punishment. Forbearing to use coercion in such cases would not increase the violations of the rights of all, as would the elimination of punishment, but would simply remove one of those violations. More fruitfully, similar considerations might be applied to other kinds of societal institutions. It would be worthwhile to inquire, for example, into the effect of alternative forms of taxation—income tax, sales tax, property tax, per capita tax—on individual rights. Clearly, different kinds of taxation affect individuals differently, and some forms appear to pose a more direct threat to individual rights than do others.[18]

The example of punishment has shown, I believe, that coercion can be justified, subject to certain constraints, and that coercive institutions not only do not illegitimately infringe individual rights but are necessary for the defense of those rights. The argument of the present work begins with the notion of individual rights; it would be possible, of course, to begin elsewhere among basic moral concepts. But since the most direct challenge to the moral justifiability of coercion arises from the concept of rights, they have furnished a useful starting point here. Coercion is wrong, I have argued, because of its interference with the rights of moral persons; at the same time, coercion is not only permissible but morally obligatory, as an element of certain social institutions, if the rights of moral persons are to be adequately protected.

Notes

1. These are among numerous defining conditions mentioned by Hobbes, in *Leviathan* (1651), part 2, chap. 28; ed. C. B. MacPherson (Baltimore: Penguin Books, 1968), 353–63; ed. Michael

Oakeshott (Oxford: Blackwell, 1960), 202–9. They are also mentioned by Rawls in "Two Concepts of Rules," *Philosophical Review* 64 (January 1955): 3–32; reprinted in John Stuart Mill, *Utilitarianism: Text and Critical Essays*, ed. Samuel Gorovitz (Indianapolis: The Bobbs-Merrill Co., 1971), 175–94, at p. 179. It should be noted that my concern in this chapter is with legal punishment, not with punishment as it may be exercised in the family or in other systems apart from a system of law and adjudication. It might be a fruitful undertaking to extend theories of punishment in the state to the practice of punishment in other contexts (the family, schools, voluntary organizations, the military), but I shall not attempt that here.

2. Classic defenses of the deterrent view of punishment include Cesare Beccaria, *On Crimes and Punishment* (1764), trans. Henry Paolucci (Indianapolis: The Bobbs-Merrill Co., 1963); and Jeremy Bentham, *An Introduction to the Principles of Morals and Legislation* (1789) (New York: Hafner Publishing Co., 1948).

3. I know of no sources which take this as the principal justification of punishment. Bentham explicitly includes it in his statement of the goal of deterrence: see chap. 13, n. 1 (pp. 170–71); chap. 15, para. xviii–xix (pp. 196–97). In Bentham as elsewhere the goal of incapacitation is prominent in discussion of capital punishment.

4. This view seems to be relatively modern. One version is defended by A. C. Ewing in *The Morality of Punishment* (London: Kegan Paul, Ltd., 1929); emphasis is on the role of punishment in moral education. Rehabilitative arguments have recently been put forward by a great many psychologists and psychiatrists. See, for example, Karl Menninger, *The Crime of Punishment* (New York: Viking Press, 1968); B. F. Skinner, *Science and Human Behavior* (New York: Macmillan Publishing Co., 1953). Skinner's behavioristic psychology is not shared by Menninger or most other defenders of the rehabilitative theory, however. Bentham, it might be noted, explicitly rejects the rehabilitative argument: see *Principles of Morals and Legislation*, chap. 15, para. xxv (pp. 200–201).

5. Utilitarian considerations may also be urged in favor of the rehabilitative view, however, if stress is placed on the benefit done both to the criminal and to society by his reform.

6. The classic statement of the retributive theory is in Immanuel Kant, *The Metaphysics of Morals* (1797), trans. H. B. Nisbet, in Hans Reiss, ed., *Kant's Political Writings* (Cambridge: Cambridge University Press, 1971), esp. section 49. Other retributive accounts of punishment are found in G. W. F. Hegel, *Philosophy of Right* (1821), trans. T. M. Knox (Oxford: Oxford University Press, 1942); and Bernard Bosanquet, *The Philosophical Theory of the State* (London: The Macmillan Co., Ltd., 1923).

7. James V. McConnell, "Criminals Can Be Brainwashed—Now," *Psychology Today* 3, no. 6 (June 1970): 14–18, 74. McConnell adds, reassuringly: "The legal and moral issues raised by such procedures are frighteningly complex, but surely we know by now that there are no simple answers."

8. Among discussions of the objections to this view, see Herbert Morris, "Persons and Punishment," *The Monist* 52, no. 4 (October 1978): 475–501, reprinted in A. I. Melden, ed., *Human Rights* (Belmont, Calif.: Wadsworth Publishing Co., 1970), 111–34; C. S. Lewis, "The Humanitarian Theory of Punishment," in *God in the Dock: Essays on Theology and Ethics*, ed. Walter Hooper (Grand Rapids, Mich.: William B. Eerdmans, 1970), 287–95; Jeffrie Murphy, *Retribution, Justice, and Therapy* (Dordrecht, Netherlands: D. Reidel, 1979), esp. part 3, "Therapeutic Intervention"; Joel Feinberg, "Crime, Clutchability, and Individuated Treatment," in *Doing and Deserving* (Princeton: Princeton University Press, 1972), 252–71. A fuller discussion of these arguments is contained in my article, "The Right to Punish and the Right to Be Punished," in H. Gene Blocker and Elizabeth Smith, ed., *John Rawls' Theory of Social Justice: An Introduction* (Athens: Ohio University Press, 1980).

9. McConnell, "Criminals Can Be Brainwashed," 74.

10. See Marshall Cohen, "Liberalism and Disobedience," *Philosophy and Public Affairs* 1, no. 3 (Spring 1972): 283–314; Rawls, *A Theory of Justice* (Cambridge: Harvard University Press, 1971), sections 55–59. Carl Cohen in *Civil Disobedience* (New York: Columbia University Press, 1971) offers an extensive but, I believe, imprecise discussion of the theory of punishment in its application to civil disobedience.

11. A deterrence theorist, T. M. Scanlon has suggested in response to an earlier draft of this chapter, need not be a crude utilitarian but might accept some principle such as the right to equal treatment under a known law, which would rule out punishment of the innocent and would set bounds, at least, on the punishments that could be imposed in particular cases for the sake of

public example. It does not appear to be necessary to accept the retributive theory of punishment, then, in order to rule out such cases.

But such a principle cannot itself be defended as the most efficient way of achieving deterrence; we are considering, *ex hypothesi*, cases in which exemplary punishment would have a significant deterrent effect. To accept this principle, therefore, is to recognize other moral considerations—based on the status and rights of persons, for example—as taking precedence over the aim of deterrence. But this is a rather mixed form of the deterrent defense of punishment: in effect, it is a defense which permits the pursuit of deterrence subject to certain constraints which themselves have a different aim.

The account I will offer below is in some ways similar, since I will argue that deterrence is a legitimate goal which may be pursued only subject to certain crucial moral constraints. I will argue, however, that certain of these constraints—in particular, those having to do with proportionality and responsibility—are essentially retributive.

12. H. L. A. Hart, "Prolegomenon to the Principles of Punishment," in *Punishment and Responsibility* (Oxford: Oxford University Press, 1968), 8–13. In my article, "The Right to Punish and the Right to Be Punished," I argue for a similar distinction between the justification of the existence of an institution of punishment and the justification of its application to individuals, employing a version of Rawls's hypothetical contract argument.

13. If, in a particular case, we were to find that the quantity of suffering imposed substantially exceeded that prevented, this claim might not stand. Perhaps we ought then to do away with the institution of punishment. But this would be evidence of one of two facts: either the institution of punishment in question is wantonly cruel, inflicting far more suffering than is necessary or justified; or the population is virtually immune to influence by threats. I assume that neither situation need obtain in normal cases.

14. As was mentioned above, I intend the term "suffering" to include legal deprivations of any kind: fines, imprisonment, parole supervision, restrictions of certain kinds of activity, and the like. Certainly it is not necessary that punishment involve any physical suffering, nor is there any reason why a retributive theory should require this.

15. The possibility of such an institution, and its consequences for the justification of punishment, were suggested to me by Frederick Stoutland. He is not to be blamed, however, for its fiendish details.

16. "The act does not make the actor guilty unless the mind is guilty also." For explanation and discussion of the *mens rea* requirement, see Glanville Williams, *The Mental Element in Crime* (Jerusalem: Magnes Press, 1965), chap. 1; Anthony Kenny, *Freewill and Responsibility* (London: Routledge and Kegan Paul, 1978).

17. Richard Wasserstrom's article, "Punishment," in *Philosophy and Social Issues* (Notre Dame: University of Notre Dame Press, 1980), 112–52, forcefully defends this point: a justification of the institution of punishment requires not merely general reasons why such an institution is desirable on the whole but also reasons why punishment is rightfully imposed in each individual case.

18. I have discussed some of the philosophical issues surrounding alternative forms of taxation in "Two Dogmas About Taxation," in Michael Bradie and David Braybrooke, eds., *Social Justice: Bowling Green Studies in Applied Philosophy*, Vol. *IV* (1982).

BIBLIOGRAPHY

Aristotle. *Nicomachean Ethics.* Translated by W. D. Ross. In *Aristotle's Ethics*, edited by J. L. Ackrill. New York: Humanities Press, 1973.

Ayer, A. J. *Language, Truth, and Logic.* New York: Dover, 1952.

Barker, Ernest. *Principles of Political and Social Theory.* Oxford: Clarendon Press, 1951.

Bay, Christian. *The Structure of Freedom.* Stanford: Stanford University Press, 1958.

Bayles, Michael. "A Concept of Coercion." In *Coercion* (*Nomos* Vol. 14), edited by Pennock and Chapman, pp. 16–29.

Beccaria, Cesare. *On Crimes and Punishment.* Translated by Henry Paolucci. Indianapolis: The Bobbs-Merrill Co., 1963.

Benn, Stanley I. "Rights." In *The Encyclopedia of Philosophy*, edited by Paul Edwards. New York: Macmillan and The Free Press, 1967.

Benn, Stanley, and Richard S. Peters. *Social Principles and the Democratic State.* London: Allen and Unwin, Ltd., 1959.

Bentham, Jeremy. *An Introduction to the Principles of Morals and Legislation.* New York: Hafner Publishing Co., 1948.

Berlin, Isaiah. *Four Essays on Liberty.* New York: Oxford University Press, 1969.

Blocker, H. Gene, and Elizabeth Smith, eds. *John Rawls' Theory of Social Justice: An Introduction.* Athens: Ohio University Press, 1980.

Bosanquet, Bernard. *The Philosophical Theory of the State.* London: The Macmillan Co., Ltd., 1923.

Brandt, Richard, ed. *Social Justice.* Englewood Cliffs, N.J.: Prentice-Hall, 1962.

———. *Ethical Theory.* Englewood Cliffs, N.J.: Prentice-Hall, 1959.

Bronaugh, Richard N. "Freedom as the Absence of an Excuse." *Ethics* 74, no. 3 (April 1964): 163.

Cohen, Carl. *Civil Disobedience.* New York: Columbia University Press, 1971.

Cohen, Marshall. "Liberalism and Disobedience." *Philosophy and Public Affairs* 1, no. 3 (Spring 1972): 283–314.

Dahl, Robert. *Modern Political Analysis.* 2d ed. Englewood Cliffs, N.J.: Prentice-Hall, 1970.

Daniels, Norman. *Reading Rawls.* New York: Basic Books, 1976.

Davidson, Donald. "How Is Weakness of Will Possible?" In *Moral Concepts*, edited by Joel Feinberg.

Duncan-Jones, Austin. "Freedom to Do Otherwise." *Cambridge Journal* 3, no. 12 (September 1950): 753.

Dworkin, Gerald. "Acting Freely." *Nous* 4, no. 4 (November 1970): 367–83.

———. "Compulsion and Moral Concepts." *Ethics* 78, no. 3 (April 1968): 227–33.

Dworkin, Ronald. "The Original Position." *Chicago Law Review* 40, no. 3 (Spring 1973): 500–533. Reprinted in Norman Daniels, ed. *Reading Rawls.*

Ewing, A. C. *The Morality of Punishment.* London: Kegan Paul, Ltd., 1929.

Fain, Haskell. "Prediction and Constraint." *Mind* 67 (1958): 372.

Feinberg, Joel. "The Nature and Value of Rights." *Journal of Value Inquiry* 4, no. 4 (Winter 1970): 243–57; reprinted in *Rights, Justice, and the Bounds of Liberty.* Princeton: Princeton University Press, 1980.

———. *Doing and Deserving.* Princeton: Princeton University Press, 1972.

———, editor. *Moral Concepts.* Oxford: Oxford University Press, 1969.

Frankena, William. "The Concept of Universal Human Rights." Paper presented at symposium, American Philosophical Association. *Science, Language, and Human Rights.* Philadelphia: University of Pennsylvania Press, 1952.

———. *Ethics.* 2d ed. Englewood Cliffs, N.J.: Prentice-Hall, 1973.

Frankfurt, Harry. "Coercion and Moral Responsibility." In *Essays on Freedom of Action,* edited by Ted Honderich.

———. "Three Concepts of Free Action." (Response to Don Locke on the same topic.) *The Aristotelian Society Supplement* 49 (1975): 113–25.

Gert, Bernard. "Coercion and Freedom." In *Coercion (Nomos* Vol. 14), edited by Pennock and Chapman, pp. 30–48.

———. *The Moral Rules.* New York: Harper & Row, 1973.

Godwin, William. *Enquiry Concerning Political Justice.* Toronto: University of Toronto Press, 1946.

Grey, Thomas C. *The Legal Enforcement of Morality.* New York: Alfred A. Knopf, 1983.

Gross, Hyman. *A Theory of Criminal Justice.* Oxford: Oxford University Press, 1979.

Hart, H. L. A. "Are There Any Natural Rights?" *Philosophical Review* 64 (1955): 175–91. Reprinted in *Political Philosophy,* edited by Anthony Quinton.

———. *Punishment and Responsibility.* Oxford: Oxford University Press, 1968.

Hayek, F. A. *The Constitution of Liberty.* Chicago: University of Chicago Press, 1960.

Hegel, G. W. F. *Philosophy of Right.* Translated by T. M. Knox. Oxford: Oxford University Press, 1942.

Held, Virginia. "Coercion and Coercive Offers." In *Coercion (Nomos* Vol. 14), edited by Pennock and Chapman, pp. 49–62.

Hill, Thomas E., Jr. "Servility and Self-Respect." *The Monist* 57, no. 1 (January 1973): 87–104.

Hobbes, Thomas. *Leviathan*. Edited by C. B. MacPherson. Baltimore: Penguin Books, 1968. Edited by Michael Oakeshott. Oxford: Blackwell, 1960.

Hoekema, David A. "The Moral Status of Nuclear Deterrent Threats." *Social Philosophy and Policy* 3, No. 1 (Autumn 1985): pp. 93–117.

———. "The Right to Punish and the Right to Be Punished." In *John Rawls' Theory of Social Justice: An Introduction*, edited by Blocker and Smith.

Hohfeld, Wesley. *Fundamental Legal Conceptions*. New Haven: Yale University Press, 1923.

Honderich, Ted, editor. *Essays on Freedom of Action*. Boston: Routledge and Kegan Paul, 1973.

Kant, Immanuel. *The Doctrine of Virtue*. Part 2 of *The Metaphysics of Morals*, edited by M. J. MacGregor. New York: Harper & Row, 1964.

———. *The Metaphysical Elements of Justice*. Part 1 of *The Metaphysics of Morals*. Translated by John Ladd. Indianapolis: Bobbs-Merrill, 1965.

———. *The Metaphysics of Morals*. Translated by H. B. Nisbet. In *Kant's Political Writings*, edited by Hans Reiss. Cambridge: Cambridge University Press, 1971.

Kavka, Gregory. "Some Paradoxes of Deterrence." *Journal of Philosophy* 75, no. 6 (June 1978): 285–302.

Kenny, Anthony. *Freewill and Responsibility*. London: Routledge and Kegan Paul, 1978.

Knight, Frank. "Freedom as Fact and Criterion." In *Freedom and Reform: Essays in Economics and Social Philosophy*. New York: Harper Brothers, 1947.

Lewis, C. S. "The Humanitarian Theory of Punishment." In *God in the Dock: Essays on Theology and Ethics*, edited by Walter Hooper. Grand Rapids, Mich.: William B. Eerdmans, 1970.

Locke, John. *Essay Concerning Human Understanding*. Edited by Alexander C. Fraser. New York: Dover, 1959.

Lucas, John Randolph. *The Principles of Politics*. New York: Oxford University Press, 1966.

Mabbott, J. D. *The State and the Citizen*. London: Arrow, 1958.

Maximoff, G. P., ed. *The Political Philosophy of Bakunin*. Glencoe, Ill.: Free Press, 1953.

MacCallum, Gerald. "Positive and Negative Freedom." *Philosophical Review* 76, no. 3 (July 1967): 314.

Melden, A. I., ed. *Human Rights*. Belmont, Calif.: Wadsworth Publishing Co., 1970.

———. *Rights and Persons*. Berkeley: University of California Press, 1977.

Menninger, Karl. *The Crime of Punishment*. New York: Viking Press, 1968.

Mill, John Stuart. *On Liberty*. Edited by Currin V. Shields. Indianapolis: The Bobbs-Merrill Co., 1956.

———. *Utilitarianism: Text and Critical Essays*. Edited by Samuel Gorovitz. Indianapolis: the Bobbs-Merrill Co., 1971.

Morgenbesser, Sidney, Patrick Suppes, and Morton White, eds. *Philosophy, Science, and Method: Essays in Honor of Ernest Nagel*. New York: St. Martin's Press, 1969.

Morris, Herbert. "Persons and Punishment." *Monist* 52, no. 4 (October 1968): 475–501. In A. I. Melden, ed. *Human Rights*.

Murphy, Jeffrey, ed. *Punishment and Rehabilitation*. Belmont, Calif.: Wadsworth Publishing Co., 1973.

———. *Retribution, Justice, and Therapy*. Dordrecht, Netherlands: D. Reidel, 1979.

Nozick, Robert. "Coercion." In *Philosophy, Science, and Method*, edited by Morgenbesser, Suppes, and White.

Oppenheim, Felix. *Dimensions of Freedom*. New York: St. Martin's Press, 1961.

Pennock, J. Roland, and John W. Chapman, eds. *Coercion* (*Nomos* Vol. 14). Chicago: Aldine Atherton Co., 1972.

Quinton, Anthony, ed. *Political Philosophy*. Oxford: Oxford University Press, 1967.

Rawls, John. "Two Concepts of Rules." *Philosophical Review* 64 (January 1955): 3–32.

———. *A Theory of Justice*. Cambridge: Harvard University Press, 1971.

Ross, W. D. *The Right and the Good*. Oxford: The Clarendon Press, 1930.

Scanlon, T. M. "Preference and Urgency." *Journal of Philosophy* 72, no. 19 (6 November 1975): pp. 655–69.

Schelling, Thomas. *The Strategy of Conflict*. Oxford: Oxford University Press, 1960.

Simmons, A. John. *Moral Principles and Political Obligations*. Princeton: Princeton University Press, 1979.

Skinner, B. F. *Science and Human Behavior*. New York: Macmillan Publishing Co., 1953.

Sobel, J. Howard. "The Need for Coercion." In *Coercion* (*Nomos* Vol. 14), edited by Pennock and Chapman, pp. 148–177.

United Nations General Assembly. *United Nations Declaration of the Rights of the Child*. In *Having Children*, edited by Onora O'Neill and William Ruddick. New York: Oxford University Press, 1979.

Vlastos, Gregory. "Justice and Equality." In *Human Rights*, edited by A. I. Melden.

Wasserstrom, Richard. "Punishment." In *Philosophy and Social Issues*. Notre Dame: University of Notre Dame Press, 1980.

———. "Rights, Human Rights, and Racial Discrimination," In *Human Rights*, edited by A. I. Melden.

Weber, Max. *The Theory of Social and Economic Organization*. Translated by A. M. Henderson and Talcott Parsons. New York: The Free Press, 1947.

Williams, Glanville. *The Mental Element in Crime*. Jerusalem: Magnes press, 1965.

INDEX